D0558792

Common Sense Catechesis

Common Sense
Catechesis

Lessons from the Past,

Road Map for the Future

Fr. Robert J. Hater

Our Sunday Visitor Publishing Division
Our Sunday Visitor, Inc.
Huntington, Indiana 46750

Nihil Obstat
Msgr. Michael Heintz, Ph.D.
Censor Librorum

Imprimatur
☩ Kevin C. Rhoades
Bishop of Fort Wayne-South Bend
December 23, 2013

The *Nihil Obstat* and *Imprimatur* are official declarations that a book is free from doctrinal or moral error. It is not implied that those who have granted the *Nihil Obstat* and *Imprimatur* agree with the contents, opinions, or statements expressed.

Scripture texts used in this work are taken from the *New American Bible*, except where noted, revised edition © 2010, 1991, 1986, 1970 Confraternity of Christian Doctrine, Washington, D.C., and are used by permission of the copyright owner. All rights reserved. No part of the New American Bible may be reproduced in any form without permission in writing from the copyright owner.

English translation of the *Catechism of the Catholic Church* for use in the United States of America copyright © 1994, United States Catholic Conference, Inc. — Libreria Editrice Vaticana. English translation of the *Catechism of the Catholic Church: Modifications from the Editio Typica* copyright © 1997, United States Catholic Conference, Inc. — Libreria Editrice Vaticana.

Quotations from papal and other Vatican-generated documents are copyright © Libreria Editrice Vaticana.

Excerpts from the English translation of the *General Directory for Catechesis*, copyright © 1997 by Libreria Editrice Vaticana, are used with permission. Published in the United States, 1998, by the United States Catholic Conference, Washington, D.C.

Excerpts from *National Directory for Catechesis* © 2005 United States Conference of Catholic Bishops, Washington, D.C. Used with permission. All rights reserved. No part of this work may be reproduced or transmitted in any form without the permission in writing form the copyright holder.

Every reasonable effort has been made to determine copyright holders of excerpted materials and to secure permissions as needed. If any copyrighted materials have been inadvertently used in this work without proper credit being given in one form or another, please notify Our Sunday Visitor in writing so that future printings of this work may be corrected accordingly.

Copyright © 2014 Robert J. Hater. Published 2014.

19 18 17 16 15 14   1 2 3 4 5 6 7 8 9

All rights reserved. With the exception of short excerpts for critical reviews, no part of this work may be reproduced or transmitted in any form or by any means whatsoever without permission in writing from the publisher. Contact: Our Sunday Visitor Publishing Division, Our Sunday Visitor, Inc., 200 Noll Plaza, Huntington, IN 46750; 1-800-348-2440; bookpermissions@osv.com.

ISBN: 978-1-61278-778-7 (Inventory No. X1584)
eISBN: 978-1-61278-356-7
LCCN: 2013957952

Cover design: Lindsey Riesen
Cover artwork: "Parable of the Sower," by Mike Dywelska, photographed by Bill Wittman
Interior design: Maggie Urgo

PRINTED IN THE UNITED STATES OF AMERICA

DEDICATION

I dedicate this book to Stanley and Olivia Hater, my parents, who first catechized me in the way of faith. From the time I was little, they taught me by word and example what following Jesus meant. Mom did it through her presence, love, and sacrifice for our family in our home. Dad showed us the example of a true Christian in the world as we worked alongside him in our small dry-goods store. With the wonderful Sisters of Charity who taught us at St. William's School in Cincinnati, these good Catholic adults prepared us well for the Christian life, regardless of what path our lives took. I thank them and ask God to grant them eternal rest.

"In the mystery of the incarnation, Jesus Christ is the human face of God and the divine face of humanity. The incarnation of the only Son of God is the original inculturation of God's word. The mystery of the incarnation is also the model of all evangelization."

(*National Directory for Catechesis*, 21A)

TABLE OF CONTENTS

Author's note: As I wrote this book, I had recourse to other previously published works that I had written. Sections of the book which include some of that previously published material are as follows:

— Parts of Chapter 5, The Systematic – Experiential Period, and parts of Chapter 6, Incarnational Catechesis in a Contemporary Context, have been adapted from *New Vision, New Directions, Implementing the Catechism of the Catholic Church*, Thomas More, Allen, Texas, 1994. This book is copyrighted in my name.

— Parts of Chapter 5, The Systematic – Experiential Period (pp. 185-seq.), have been adapted from a previously published article, "Advancing Excellence in Catechetical Ministry," which appeared in *The Catechetical Leader*, an NCCL publication, Vol. 15, No. 2, June 2004.

— A significant part of Chapter 6, Incarnational Catechesis in a Contemporary Context, has been adapted from a previously published article, "Incarnational Catechesis: The Word Becomes Flesh," which appeared in *The Catechetical Leader*, an NCCL publication, Vol. 17, No. 6, November/December 2008.

FOREWORD

"Each of us should find ways to communicate Jesus wherever we are. All of us are called to offer others an explicit witness to the saving love of the Lord, who despite our imperfections offers us his closeness, his word and his strength, and gives meaning to our lives."

(Pope Francis, *Evangelii Gaudium*, 121)

Fr. Robert Hater is one of the most outstanding contributors to the field of catechesis in modern times. I have been privileged to work with him while he served as the Archdiocese of Cincinnati's Director of Religious Education and later as a colleague in the Department of Religious Studies at the University of Dayton in Ohio. His creative, curious, and insightful perception of the Church and the signs of the times placed him on the cutting edge of catechetical movements within the Church. He entered the catechetical field during a time of transition and experimentation. New theories and methodologies in teaching and learning were quickly evolving. Psychology, sociology, and anthropology introduced new perspectives for understanding the human person in an evolving information age. Political seismic shifts were occurring within cultures and across nations as many sought to redefine their boundaries and identities. Secularism, relativism, consumerism, and individualism were breeding a new consciousness that challenged, or replaced, traditional values. The traditional Catholic family climate that offered balance, stability, and direction for one's faith life was being shaken from within. The impact of the Second Vatican

Council's call for a new way of being Church in the modern world was being explored with a cacophony of interpretations within every level of the Church and ministry. It is within this context that Fr. Hater emerged, bringing his practical theological knowledge and rich pastoral experiences to weave new tapestries of wisdom and insight for reimagining catechesis in the late twentieth and early twenty-first centuries.

In *Common Sense Catechesis*, Fr. Hater ingeniously crafts a historical catechetical perspective enabling us to identify alternative rationales for coming to terms with, at times, our current catechetical concerns and questions: Why is there such a loss of Catholic culture and identity within the lives of Catholics today? Why is parish participation rapidly declining? How did a vacuum of quality and depth of faith formation evolve? What factors have generated the growing ambiguity of knowledge and comprehension of Church teachings among both children and adults alike? Why are Catholics unable to clearly and convincingly explain their faith when either confronted by, or invited to engage in dialogue with, the diversity of religious traditions that surround every dimension of our lives? How do we stir into flame within all Catholics a dynamic living faith that embraces Pope Francis' call to be prophetic missionary disciples in the world? How did we get here? Yet, even more important, how do we, as catechists, turn things around, or head in a fresh new direction?

Pope Francis challenged us in his homily to catechists in this regard: "The catechist, then, is a Christian who is mindful of God, who is guided by the memory of God in his or her entire life and who is able to awaken that memory in the hearts of others. This is not easy! It engages our entire existence! What is the Catechism itself, if not the memory of God, the memory of his works in history and his drawing near to us in Christ present in his word, in the sacraments, in his Church, in his love? Dear catechists, I ask you: Are we in fact the memory of God? Are we really like sentinels who awaken in others the memory of God which warms the heart?" (September 29, 2013). *Common Sense Catechesis* is a definite response to Pope Francis' challenge. Fr. Hater boldly leads us on the journey forward.

Every catechist needs to have a historical catechetical perspective. This perspective enables catechists to learn from the past in order to re-imagine the future. This is imperative if catechists are to avoid repeating the events that created our current catechetical demise. Without overwhelming his readers with a plethora of theological or ecclesial jargon, Fr. Hater introduces his readers to the contextualizing catechetical factors that unraveled over the past sixty years. He calls these phases, or periods, of modern catechetical history. With pastoral ease he guides his readers through each phase with three key points: 1) The Historical Perspective; 2) His Personal Catechetical and Pastoral Experiences; and, 3) Trends and Results of the Period. The concise summary of the third point of each phase offers readers both clues and challenges for avoiding pitfalls of the past.

Chapters 6 and 7 are the highlights of *Common Sense Catechesis.* It is here that Fr. Hater sparks our religious imagination to discover a new approach or methodology for catechesis in the twenty-first century. He presents us with sound theological and biblical foundations that resonate with the challenges we see set before us as we continue to read the signs of the times. We clearly see that Fr. Hater is in sync with Pope Francis' articulation of the mission and vision for the new missionary discipleship of the Church. The detailed catechetical guidelines in Chapter 7 are clues for considering a new catechetical approach. This is the real gem in the book as it leads us to fresh new ideas for re-imagining catechetical processes today. A catechetical leader can feel comfortable and at ease creating a new catechetical pastoral plan of action by carefully reading, reflecting, imagining, and dialoguing with their team of catechists around the ideas clearly defined in these pages. In this light they may discover a new perspective for cultivating depth in faith formation, for nurturing an informed and knowledgeable Catholic who authentically witnesses to a living faith. The catechist is alerted that new methodologies require new techniques, and the digital culture offers catechists a vast array of digital resources. How do catechists courageously go about navigating into the digital milieu with prophetic vision and influence?

First, catechists need to realize that digital natives, young women and men who have spent copious hours engaging in virtual worlds since early childhood, are changing. Neuroscience studies indicate that knowledge is actually organized differently now because of the abundant technologies available at our fingertips. The brains of digital natives are being remapped in light of their intensive and continuous time spent with digital technologies. They think and process information differently today. New learning ecologies, or spaces and places of learning, are becoming more dominant. Individuals can learn anytime and anywhere. Catechists need to embrace the new reality and understand its influence for how, when, and where we catechize digital natives. New digital resources are not simply a show-and-tell occasional experience, or an exercise in the learning environment to entertain the learner. Digital resources must be creatively woven into the catechetical learning experience. This is dramatically different than the collage, copy and paste of past catechetical practices! We are now conscious that digital-learner brains are rewired for new learning styles.

Second, amidst a culture of distraction and an eclipse of the Great Mystery (God), catechists are called to guide those we catechize to rediscover their direction, or GPS, toward a new awakening of God in their lives. As Pope Francis says in *Evangelii Gaudium*, "Today's vast and rapid cultural changes demand that we constantly seek ways of expressing unchanging truths in a language which brings out their abiding newness" (41). This is what Fr. Hater strongly advocates and inspires catechists to realize with his challenge of a new catechetical approach — an approach solidly grounded in the teachings of the Catholic Church and animated with sound methodologies. He further reminds us that catechesis never carried the primary burden for faith formation of Catholics. The family and the whole Catholic community have roles to play; however, catechesis has a critical and crucial formative role for conveying basic truths of the faith to those to be catechized.

Throughout this book we catch glimpses of Fr. Hater's profound faith, love for the Church, and religious imagination. We are held captive by a great storyteller who is able to instill within us a great love for our vocation as catechists. We find ourselves energized to rediscover a new catechetical pathway into the future because we stand on the shoulders of faith-filled pioneers, like Fr. Hater, who dare to dream and invite us to dream with them!

Sister Angela Ann Zukowski, MHSH, D.Min.
The University of Dayton
Dayton, Ohio
November 2013

ACKNOWLEDGMENTS

I am very grateful to the people who evaluated this manuscript and offered many valuable suggestions to make it a better text. These include: Colleen Gerke, Director of the Family and Respect Life Office, Archdiocese of Cincinnati; Sr. Marilyn Kerber, SNDdeN, Director of the Office of Religious, Archdiocese of Cincinnati; Virginia P. Rush, Director of Religious Education, All Saints Parish, Cincinnati; and Julie St. Croix, Religious Education Staff, Archdiocese of Baltimore.

I am deeply grateful to Heidi Busse of Our Sunday Visitor for all the help she afforded me as my editor and friend to bring this book to completion. From the beginning of our work on this manuscript her professional and friendly style supported me and greatly enhanced the book. I wish to express my special gratitude to her.

I wish to express my deepest appreciation to my friend and colleague of many years, Sr. Angela Ann Zukowski, MHSH, D. Min., for writing a wonderful Foreword to *Common Sense Catechesis*. In the midst of her busy teaching and travel schedule as a pioneer in the use of digital media in catechesis, she generously agreed to take the time to read the manuscript and offer her insightful words. Special thanks to her.

INTRODUCTION

"Let us witness the newness, hope and joy that the Lord brings us."

(Pope Francis, General Audience,
May 22, 2013)

Catechesis is not about what we ourselves do, but about what God calls us to do. God called Abraham, Ruth, Moses, and David. God called Mary, His mother, Peter, Mary Magdalene, and Paul. God calls us.

After Pentecost, the disciples heard God's call and responded, transforming a world in the process. Jewish Christians followed God's call and showed how Jesus fulfilled all the messianic prophecies of the Old Law. Paul followed God's call and changed the Gentile world in light of Jesus' teachings. In each instance, they connected God's calling to proclaim the Good News with the existing culture. The same pattern has been followed from the beginning, in the Church's efforts to catechize with the spirit and vibrancy of Christ. Today, God calls us to transform our culture and move people's hearts through a new evangelization.

Early missionaries connected the Good News with the pagan cultures that they evangelized. This happened in our country when the Word of God was preached to Native American peoples and transformed them in light of the Gospels. Where this connection of the Gospel to culture was not made, little evangelization occurred.

God calls us to do the same as we face challenges similar to those encountered by missionaries of every age. To succeed, the content of the faith must be presented in a way that those to whom it is addressed can understand and accept it. This is nothing new. Seven hundred years ago, Saint Thomas Aquinas said, "Whatever is received is received according to the mode of the one receiving it." In other words, the existing environment, climate, and culture are the context within which people hear the Christian message.

For people to hear and understand the Good News, catechists must present Jesus' message in a way that connects with the situation and experience of those to whom it is addressed. This means that their secular environment must be considered. The message must be presented in such a way that they understand it and apply it to the challenges coming from the secular world.

Twenty-first-century catechists are to teach the Christian message in a way that takes into account new media, technological advances, the secular culture, and our relativistic world, and presents it with the modes of communication that postmodern people use. This means that catechists relate Christian teachings to the media-savvy world in which they live. As Pope Francis says in *Evangelii Gaudium*, "Today's vast and rapid cultural changes demand that we constantly seek ways of expressing unchanging truths in a language which brings out their abiding newness" (41).

Digital technology is changing society. It's shifting how we think and act. In the midst of this revolution, catechesis must change. If not, the Word of God will go unheard by countless people around the world.

As we look to the future and ask what these changes will entail, we must also remember the past. From history, we learn important lessons, as new methods and ways of catechizing emerge. Consequently, this book begins with a challenge. Can we get insights into the new catechetical directions from what has happened after Vatican II?

This concern about new media does not imply watering down basic Catholic beliefs. It means making sure that they connect with contemporary issues found in the home and at work. This is the task of the New Evangelization. If it is not done as catechists teach about Jesus and His love, basic Church teachings will strike deaf ears.

The timeless truths of the faith never change, but the style of the new catechesis in a postmodern world must change. As recent popes have called for a new evangelization, this book calls for a new catechesis, a "common sense catechesis."

To appreciate the new catechesis, we root this book in a historical perspective and in my own catechetical journey over the past sixty years. These provide a framework to consider past accomplishments, future hopes, and the burning issue of how to effectively catechize. This approach analyzes the factors that influenced catechesis and how they disclose the larger context of what happened after Vatican II. It uses history and my catechetical journey as a window into the new world of catechesis in the culture of the United States.

Effective catechesis is always framed by culture. The way that the Church responds to new challenges influences how God's Word is received. To address these challenges, we keep in mind the directions that flow from the *General Directory for Catechesis*, the U.S. bishops' Subcommittee on the Catechism, and other Church documents. To discover what these new directions portend for catechesis, we begin by examining catechetical approaches from before Vatican II and trace them to the present.

The book is divided into seven chapters. Chapter 1 sets the foundations for *Common Sense Catechesis* by analyzing the Catholic culture and clarifying necessary terminology used in the book. The other chapters describe periods of catechesis during the past 125 years.

Chapter 2 describes a stable, firmly grounded Church and the Systematic – Memorization Period (first part of the twentieth century). This first period began in the latter part of the nineteenth century after the Third Plenary Council of Baltimore (1884). After that council, the *Baltimore Catechism* became the norm for catechizing Catholics. This period extended until after Vatican II.

Chapter 3 treats the inductive Eclectic – Chaotic Period (late 1960s to 1980). This second period started around 1968 when reactions to the reforms of Vatican II catalyzed a widespread rejection of the *Baltimore Catechism's* approach to teaching religion. In its wake a catechetical no man's land developed where much experimentation began to take place.

Chapter 4 considers the Experiential – Systematic Period (1980s to 1990s). This third period took shape about 1975. It began concurrently with the increased use of the Rite of Christian Initiation of Adults (RCIA). As the third millennium approached, liturgical catechesis, influenced by a faith-sharing perspective, received more attention. In 1994, the pope and bishops approved *the Catechism of the Catholic Church.* Initially, it received mixed reviews from those advocating newer ways to catechize, but its promulgation marked the beginning of a new era.

Chapter 5 analyzes the Systematic – Experiential Period (2000 to the present). This fourth period began around 1995 and developed further in the first decade of the third millennium. Influenced by the publication of the *Catechism of the Catholic Church,* and the *General Directory for Catechesis,* this period centered catechesis on the basic teachings of the Catholic faith and reaffirmed the best catechetical approaches that emerged after Vatican II.

Chapter 6 considers incarnational catechesis in light of the Christology coming from Vatican II, which set the theological foundation for renewing catechesis. It also addresses the challenges coming from the secular world, and the assistance catechists receive through the bishops' Subcommittee on the Catechism.

Chapter 7 proposes a new approach to catechesis called "Common Sense Catechesis." It can also be called the Systematic – Personalistic Approach. The chapter introduces it, gives an example of how it works, and offers further reflections. This approach emphasizes basic Church teachings and using the best approaches to catechesis developed during the last twenty-five years of the second millennium. Insights coming from the International Synod of Bishops on the New Evangelization in Rome in October 2012 are incorporated into *Common Sense Catechesis.* The New Evangelization offers the seeds for a balanced and complete perspective on catechesis.

The Conclusion offers hope as a new era in catechesis dawns.

CHAPTER 1

SETTING THE FOUNDATION

"Spreading the Gospel means that we are ... first to proclaim and live the reconciliation, forgiveness, peace, unity, and love which the Holy Spirit gives us."

(Pope Francis, *General Audience*, May 22, 2013)

Catechesis echoes the Good News of Jesus' love and forgiveness. Christians always shared His message. During times of freedom and oppression, Jesus' message brought hope and inspired courage. This is needed in our time, as society struggles to find meaning in a secular environment.

Today's catechists need to make clear Jesus' message and the Church's basic beliefs and practices as they take seriously the cultural context and the life experience of the catechized. They must also utilize biblical catechesis and storytelling, and employ effective, catechetical approaches, including new technological and digital tools. Catechists must recognize catechesis as an effective mode of evangelization, emphasize adult faith formation, and see parents as co-catechizers. Their challenge is to integrate catechesis into the broader context of parish ministry.

Digital technology is central in the new catechetical enterprise. It shifts how we think and act. In the midst of this revolution, catechesis must change. If not, the Word of God will go unheard by countless people around the world.

As we look to future changes in catechesis, we must remember the past. Catechesis is different now than when Archbishop Joseph Bernardin invited me to begin the Cincinnati Religious Education Office in 1973.

Many people malign the years after the Second Vatican Council for their failure to teach the basics of the Catholic Church. Some catechists used methods that centered on human experience and minimized basic Church teachings. In today's era of digital catechesis, we use new methods, centered on twenty-first-century technology. Will this era also minimize basic Church teachings? Will catechists pick and choose what to teach? Will they concentrate more on how to teach technologically than stressing the basic Church teachings which our bishops strongly recommend?

Reasons for ambiguity in catechesis following Vatican II rest largely on the changes in the Catholic climate. Catechetical uncertainty extended from faithful Catholics to parishes, diocesan offices, and the hierarchy. The latter struggled to deal with the complex and challenging issues of the time, as the Church began to implement the council's directives. This often involved reducing tensions in parishes, dioceses, and the wider Church. Strong feelings surfaced over issues such as what and how to teach children, sex education, and changes in the Mass. There were also many disagreements over experimental liturgies, priests and nuns leaving religious life, artificial birth control, the Vietnam War, student protests on campuses, civil rights, women's rights, and social action.

This chapter is divided into two main sections. The first addresses the changing Catholic climate after Vatican II. The second clarifies the terminology used in this book.

Section 1:
A CHANGING CATHOLIC CLIMATE

We begin by looking at the Catholic culture and the Catholic climate, because these play major roles in the success of catechesis.

The heart of our reflections centers on the Catholic climate. It's important to note, first of all, that "Catholic climate" is not the same as "Catholic culture." "Catholic culture" does not necessarily include the psychological and emotional aspects that "Catholic climate" includes. For example, at any given time and place in history, "Catholic culture" embraces core Catholic beliefs and practices. In this sense, people of various ethnic cultures embrace the same Catholic culture.

Nuanced differences exist within the broader Catholic culture of every time and place. Consider the deanery where your parish is located. It consists of a variety of parishes — large, small, Anglo and ethnic, well-established and newly formed. Some of these parishes are merged from several parishes and work together as a parish cluster. Each reflects the core Catholic culture in its beliefs and practices. All parishes operate under the leadership of the pope and the local bishop. All have an ordained priest-pastor. They share the same seven sacraments and profess the same creed and beliefs. In this sense, the core Catholic culture in these parishes is the same as it is in Africa, Asia, and throughout the world.

On the other hand, parishes differ from one other. Their differences reflect variants in the "Catholic climate." In a deanery, one parish may be alive with beautiful music, activities, vibrant youth programs, effective catechesis, social ministry, and a pastor able to inspire his congregation. The neighboring parish may reflect little life and have people leaving to join other parishes or evangelical denominations. This may result from ineffective homilies, poorly planned liturgies, weak pastoral leadership, or a host of other factors. Both parishes have the same core Catholic culture, but the climate of each is different. The same applies to a single parish that at one time had a pastor who inspired, led, and motivated the congregation. When he left and was replaced by another pastor who changed things and stifled the life of the congregation, things changed significantly. In other words, the core Catholic culture remained, but the Catholic climate changed. Something similar exists as various ethnic cultures affect Catholic climate.

From the above descriptions, we see that "Catholic climate" refers to the way that Catholic beliefs and practices in any cultural and historical time are received and filtered through a Catholic community. In other words, the Catholic climate is the fundamental orientation of Catholics in a certain place and at a given historical time. It's easier to illustrate this than to define it, for it operates largely in the realm of the collective unconscious of Catholics. This book limits itself largely to the Catholic climate in the United States. This climate has provided the underpinning for catechesis and religious education at any given time in our country's history.

A Catholic climate exists wherever there are Catholics. Sometimes, it is stronger and more unified than at other times. Before Vatican II, it was very strong, controlled largely by living in conformity to Church teaching. Catholics were unified in their beliefs and practices.

In my childhood, our family lived in a strong, unified Catholic climate. There were no major issues concerning Catholic identity. We grew up knowing we were Catholics. We also knew we were Americans. Being Catholic was as deeply imbedded in us as being American. There was no doubt about either. Both were taken for granted.

We believed the teachings of the Church and respected the pope, bishops, clergy, nuns, and religious men and women. They were loved and held in great reverence. We used the same prayer books, said the Rosary, venerated the saints, and went to Mass and confession regularly. We received holy Communion often, even daily. We also attended religious devotions, like Our Lady of Perpetual Help novenas. We had great devotion to Mary, the Mother of God, and said prayers at home. These included morning and evening prayers. We were proud of our parish and Catholic school, which were the center of our lives outside the home. We hung around with other Catholics and were discouraged from dating non-Catholics.

Catholics came here from Italy, Germany, Ireland, and other countries, or lived here for generations. They were Catholic and American, even though they possessed different ethnic traits and sometimes didn't associate with one another. Irish Catholics often didn't get along with German Catholics. In the nineteenth century, many built their own churches within a block of each other. They knew, however, that they were Catholics. They followed the same pope and the same teaching.

The core Catholic culture held them together as Catholics. When studying in New York, a father of a boy planning to go to a Catholic university in Ohio called me aside and asked, "I've got only one question for you: Will Marco, my eldest son, meet a good Italian Catholic girl there?" For the father, being Italian and being Catholic were more important than anything else. But being Catholic transcended age, nationality, and social boundaries. Its most powerful symbols were the Latin Mass, Friday abstinence, the Lenten fast, the Rosary, and unity under the pope.

In my youth, I knew Catholics belonged to Eastern Catholic Churches, such as the Maronite or Melkite rites. While not connected in language or liturgical celebrations to the Latin (Western) Roman Catholic Church, Western- and Eastern-rite Catholics were bound to one another by their unity with Rome, and through the teachings of the Catholic Church. All were Catholics in the deepest sense.

The Catholic Church before Vatican II was a relatively closed society, immune from many pressures of secular society. When this closed society began to break down after the council, the pressures of the secular world came into the Church and affected Catholic belief and practices. Secular influences included a growing materialism and amorality. There was also a great deal of cultural unrest, pressures from the civil rights movement, the weakening of the family, drug abuse, rebellion, and the breakdown of the Catholic ghetto. The impact of all these factors on Catholic beliefs and practices is described in greater detail in Chapter 2.

The influence of secular society and the changes of Vatican II shifted the orientation of Catholics. The Catholic climate changed focus and was greatly weakened after the council. Unquestioning allegiance to the Catholic Church stopped being the underlying trait that bound all Catholics together or held them in unity with the institutional Church. Chapters 2 and 3 clarify why and how this happened.

When the Catholic climate changed, so did the rock-solid acceptance of Church teachings.

Appreciating the Catholic climate is essential to understanding Catholic identity, which never exists in the abstract. It is a constantly changing reality. It is rooted in history and grounded in basic Catholic beliefs and practices. A major reason for difficulties in catechesis today comes from the fact that the Catholic climate has changed and become greatly weakened. With it, so has Catholic identity. This book looks at Catholic identity or lack of it in each period described before or after Vatican II. By viewing Catholic identity in this way — in a historical context — we can better appreciate what happened to catechesis. Then, we can learn how to move effectively into the future.

Section 2:
CHANGING TERMINOLOGY

Just as the Catholic climate changed after Vatican II, so did the language of religious education. Eventually, the words "catechesis" and "religious formation" became popular. Before analyzing the changes that occurred in the Church, we should consider this change in terminology.

Formation in faith is not the same as imparting information. Formation is much broader, and catechesis is one component of faith formation. Initial formation in the faith happens before catechesis occurs in the parish. Faith formation begins in the family with the good example and instruction of parents. As Pope Francis says, "It is important for parents to be the first catechists, the first educators in their faith in their own families, by their witness and by their words" (*Address to International Catechetical Congress*, September 27, 2013). The witness of the parents must be supported by the parish faith community.

What is the role of catechesis? Catechesis is about formation in the faith and initiation into the Christian life. In this process, the catechist is to impart the basic teachings or content of the faith. This is an intellectual endeavor. Such knowledge is formational. When people learn the truths of the faith, these truths inform them as to how God dwells with them, and how they should respond to God and their neighbors. The good example of the catechist also is formational. So are prayer, retreats, and the sacraments. The catechist provides a role model for the one catechized. But this example never fully substitutes for the example of parents.

Chapter 2 uses the terms "religious education" and "catechesis" interchangeably. Although technically different, this difference did not come into prominence in the Catholic community until the 1970s and 1980s. In the period before Vatican II, expressions such as "studying the catechism," "learning one's religion," or "going to religion class" were commonly used. "Catechesis," "catechist," or "catechetical process" were unfamiliar terms in most parishes and Catholic schools. Although the word "catechism" was used frequently, the words "catechesis" and "catechist" were not. Chapters 3, 4, and 5 switch to the almost exclusive use of the term "catechesis." This change in terminology and in approach began in the United States in the late 1960s and continues to the present.

For the sake of clarity, we describe how "religious instruction" and "catechesis" are used today. The *General Directory for Catechesis* says that "religious instruction" is:

A scholastic discipline with the same systematic demands and the same vigor as other disciplines. It
must present the Christian message and the Christian
event with the same seriousness and the same depth
with which other disciplines present their knowledge.
It is called to penetrate a particular area of culture
and to relate to other areas of knowledge. (73)

Catechesis and religious instruction are complementary.
Catechesis focuses on formation into the Christian faith. It provides the basis for adhering to Jesus (*GDC*, 63). As an essential moment in the evangelization process, it is at the service of
Christian initiation and lays the foundation for initiation into
and growth in the faith. Presenting the basic truths of the faith
is a critical element in all catechetical endeavors. Hence, instruction in the faith is vital. After Vatican II, many catechists did not
appreciate that learning the truths of the faith is itself initiatory.

While directed toward conversion and transformation,
catechesis includes an intellectual element as a vital part of its
role in Christian initiation. It aims at "developing an understanding of the mystery of Christ in the light of God's word"
(*Catechesi Tradendae*, 20). Consequently,

catechesis is a process that invites a person to hear,
understand, interiorize, and respond to God's word
in acts of service and celebration. (Hater, *Parish Catechetical Ministry*, p. 3)

To blame poor catechesis after Vatican II for the defection
of Catholics who left the Church is woefully incomplete and
often wrong. Much more was involved. Reflecting on the past

sixty years of catechesis from my personal perspective might help to make this more clear. I also hope to offer solid directions for the future.

As far as catechesis is concerned, various approaches or methods can be employed. For our purposes, I describe two of them that have particular significance. These are the systematic and the experiential approaches.

The expression "systematic," or "systematic approach," refers to catechetical approaches that begin with the basic beliefs or messages of faith and apply them to specific Christian experiences or actions to give individuals or groups new insights about Christian ways of living. It is exemplified by the catechism approach where universal beliefs contained there are applied to specific Christian actions.

An "experiential approach" refers to catechetical methods that begin with experience (or action). This teaching method connects experience with the basic beliefs or messages of faith to give individuals or groups new insights about Christian ways of living. This is exemplified by approaches that begin by discussing human experiences and then looking at them in light of Scripture and basic Catholic beliefs. Out of this comes new insights about ways of living.

In our reflections, "approach" rather than "method" or "methodology" is used when referring to catechetical methods. "Approach" integrates both content and method, even though it focuses primarily on content. In blending both, it gets away from the dichotomy between content and method, avoids an either/or mentality, and moves toward a both/and catechetical perspective.

Regardless of the approach used, we remember that faith is a gift of God. No Catholic climate, whatever it might be, or catechetical approach, or terminology alone, can impart faith to any person. Parents alone can't do it; neither can catechists. The most they can do is to establish a strong and supportive climate where the grace of God functions. Why some children of the same family accept the faith and others reject it is part of the mystery of faith.

CHAPTER 2

SYSTEMATIC – MEMORIZATION PERIOD

(First Part of the Twentieth Century to Vatican II, 1962-1965)

"The faith is perhaps the most beautiful heritage that we can give because it makes you grow. To help boys and girls, young men, women, and adults to know and love the Lord even more is one of the most beautiful educational adventures, for it comprises the Church."

(Pope Francis, *Address to International Catechetical Congress*, September 27, 2013)

In "Help Their Unbelief," an article in the September 10-17, 2012, issue of *America* magazine, Matt Emerson comments on why students from stable Catholic homes resist or reject formation in the faith. He says, "Part of the inertia lies within Catholicism itself." After going on to explain what he means, he continues: "It is not the case, as many tend to believe (and once I did), that more or better catechesis will solve the problem. Ultimately, formation in the Catholic faith is not simply a matter of reading or memorizing or knowing a 'bunch of stuff'" (pp. 13-14).

What he says here is a key that underpins our treatment of catechesis. It is addressed in this chapter, which is divided into three sections. Section 1 gives the historical perspectives of the period, Section 2 reflects on my catechetical journey, and Section 3 analyzes the trends emerging from this period.

Section 1:
HISTORICAL PERSPECTIVES

Before the publication of the *Baltimore Catechism* in 1885, Catholic instruction had no clear format. The First Provincial Council of Baltimore recognized this, and in 1829 it decreed that a catechism be developed to fit the needs of the time. The bishops intended to adapt *Cardinal Bellarmine's Catechism* of 1529, written during the Protestant Reformation. But this never happened.

The same injunction to produce a catechism was given both at the First (1852) and Second (1866) Plenary Councils of Baltimore. After the Second Plenary Council, anti-Catholicism had grown stronger, and there was considerable opposition and bias against Catholics in some public schools.

Such prejudice strengthened the resolve of the bishops at the Third Plenary Council of Baltimore in 1884 to develop a Catholic catechism. They issued this directive and the publication of the *Catechism of Catholic Doctrine, Prepared and Enjoined by Order of the Third Council of Baltimore* followed in 1886.

This catechism's initial version received considerable criticism. It needed significant nuancing, and contained mistakes that needed to be corrected. After this was done, it was given the name *Baltimore Catechism*. Intended as the main teaching tool used by Catholics in the United States, it standardized the terminology and basic teachings of the Church, and developed them into a workable and clear synthesis. It was the Church's standard tool to teach the faith until Vatican II changes initiated new approaches to teaching religion.

The Third Plenary Council of Baltimore decreed that every parish should have a Catholic school, to which Catholics were obliged to send their children. Sometimes, parents were denied Communion at Mass if they did not abide by this directive. The publication of the *Baltimore Catechism* and the requirement to attend Catholic schools were major forces that moved the Catholic faith in the United States into the strong position that it occupied before Vatican II.

Before the publication of the *Baltimore Catechism*, Catholics used various books in Catholic religious education. Benziger Brothers Press published a standard series that was widely used in Catholic schools. This series included textbooks on various subjects such as mathematics, reading, and grammar. The *Third Reader* of the Catholic National Series, written by Rt. Rev. Richard Gilmore, DD, Bishop of Cleveland, is an example. This was a grammar book, not a religion book. Nonetheless, the cover page of this grammar book described the publishers as "Printers to the Holy Apostolic See."

In the 1940s and 1950s, Catholic publishers issued book series in various subjects, such as English and history. These books contained religious lessons for elementary and secondary Catholic school students. This was prior to the time when Catholic schools received free textbooks from the state. Catholic high school textbooks in subjects like algebra and history, still in my bookcase, are permeated with Catholic stories and values.

A number of secular publishers also published Catholic books on grammar, mathematics, and history that contained stories of faith for lessons in various disciplines. As a whole, these books proposed basic beliefs of the Catholic faith in indirect, though inspiring, stories. All were told in textbooks that addressed "secular subjects"! Even some secular publishers of mathematics and other subjects developed a "Catholic" edition for use in Catholic schools. This format lasted until various states began providing textbooks for Catholic schools.

When Catholic schools began getting free textbooks from the state, Catholic publishers of secular subjects and secular publishers that provided Catholic editions of secular subjects often faded from the scene. In time, books used in Catholic schools became totally secular except for religion books used in religion classes.

In the 1950s and 1960s, the seeds were sown for a change in focus regarding the way religious education was taught. This began to be felt more intently in the 1960s when the spirit of change burst into full bloom during and after Vatican II.

Section 2:
MY CATECHETICAL JOURNEY

My story falls into the larger perspectives just described. From before the Third Plenary Council of Baltimore (1884) until after Vatican II, religious instruction and formation happened in a holistic way in Catholic schools. Its values were evident in the stories and examples in Catholic books on every subject even though those books lacked the specific theological nuances that the catechism presented. What was taught was enriched by statues and crucifixes hanging on classroom walls, by the religious women who taught the classes, and by the overall atmosphere of prayer that permeated the school. Achievements in school were often rewarded with holy cards of Jesus, Mary, or the saints. These schools were part of a neighborhood that was largely Catholic.

Religious formation took place in a relatively closed Catholic community. Almost everything in my neighborhood was "Catholic." When people asked where we were from, we said "St. William's Parish," not "Cincinnati." This happened in many other places as well.

Where Catholics were in the minority, their Catholicism still formed the basis for their decision-making. It was reflected in the Catholic climate and the faith that existed in their homes. Families prayed together, hung crucifixes and holy pictures on the walls, and placed statues on bookcases in bedrooms and other places. Parents brought their children to Mass on Sundays, and to other religious observances during the week.

The home was the locus of Catholic identity. Following this was the parish and the Catholic elementary school, if one existed. The parish and school were hubs of activity beyond the home. Sunday life centered on going to Mass. No one deliberately missed it, fearing punishment in the eternal flames of hell. This fear also moved Catholics to avoid servile work and not shop on Sundays. Stores were closed except for small delicatessens or restaurants. The drugstore down the street was only open until 1:00 p.m.

Elementary School

In my childhood, neighborhood Catholic children and teenagers played in the schoolyard after school, on Saturdays, and during the summer. Many were on church-sponsored sports teams. Large religious statues stood on church grounds. Priests and sisters showed up in the schoolyard after school to talk to the children, or play ball with us. We respected and admired them as God's direct representatives. We worked at the bingo games on Tuesdays, after we went to the novena in church. Sometimes, we participated in church processions.

As children, the ritual for beginning class each day was the same. We assembled in our classroom at about 8:00 a.m. We prayed, and then went immediately to Mass. Our parish, typical in size for this predominately Catholic area, celebrated daily Masses at 6:00, 6:30, 7:00, 7:30, 8:00, and 8:30 a.m. At the last three Masses, three priests began distributing holy Communion immediately after the consecration to take care of the large numbers of daily Mass attendees who came to receive Communion before each Mass ended and the next one began. The priests distributed Hosts previously consecrated at an earlier Mass. During one Forty Hours weekend (three days long), the parish used about 10,000 hosts.

After Mass, the students returned to their classrooms and religion classes began. These classes generally included answering catechism questions that the teacher assigned to be memorized for our homework the day before.

As class began, we usually formed a large circle around the classroom. The sister called on one student at a time, and asked a catechism question. If we answered correctly, we remained standing. If not, we sat down in our seats. The teacher went from student to student, around the circle. Eventually, after most students missed, the teacher returned to earlier questions we had previously learned. Finally, the one student who remained standing won the prize, usually a holy card. Religion teachers used this memorization method whether they taught in Catholic schools or Confraternity of Christian Doctrine (CCD) classes. CCD classes were usually held once a week in parishes for students attending public schools.

Ask Catholics in their sixties and older, "Who made you?" and most will still answer, "God made me." Ask, "Why did God make you?" you will get the answer, "To know Him, to love Him, and to serve Him in this world, and to be happy with Him forever in heaven." Try asking, "What is a sacrament?" The reply usually is, "A sacrament is an outward sign, instituted by Christ to give grace." Sometimes, to give us a break, the teacher read biblical quotes, taught us about the saints, or used a Catholic comic book in class.

When walking home for lunch, some students stopped in church for a visit to the Blessed Sacrament. They bowed their heads, made the Sign of the Cross, and took off their hats when going past church doors to honor Jesus in the Blessed Sacrament. Some grade school and high school students attended the Stations of the Cross after school, before they went home for the day.

Religious instruction pictured God as loving, but also to be feared. We feared eternal damnation for unforgiven mortal sins. This fear sometimes led us to see God as a stern judge. Personal guilt was part of our Catholic mentality. This brought on scrupulosity and weekly confessions for many Catholics. We often pictured God as distant and unapproachable. He was above and beyond us. We were not encouraged to form a personal relationship with Jesus. He was the divine Son of God, and we were merely human. How could we have a personal relationship with Him?

We received first Communion and were confirmed in the second grade. Both were special times, as was Corpus Christi, when a long procession wound around the church and went outside into the neighborhood. Even frequenters of the saloon across from the church came out of the bar to listen to the singing and watch the procession. As we grew up, boys served at Mass and sang in the choir. Our parish was "totally Catholic." It rubbed off on us.

We received holy Communion on our tongues, we never touched the Host. In some parishes, communicants knelt with their hands under a white cloth. It was considered a sin to touch the Host, and we were careful that no particles of the Host fell on the floor. We fasted from midnight of the night before, and drank no water before Communion. The day that I received my first Communion, our teacher wrapped heavy cloth around the water fountains so that we could not drink water before Mass if we forgot. Such symbols of the Catholic faith spoke more loudly about basic beliefs and attitudes than what we learned in religion books. We recognized the divinity of Christ, but it was not so easy to recognize His humanity, or develop a relationship with Him as our friend.

Mary, the mother of God, played a prominent part in Catholic life. We said the Rosary often, put statues of Mary in our homes and classrooms, and read beautiful verses about Mary that the teacher put around the blackboard on her feasts. The May Crowning was a highlight of the school year. An eighth-grade girl, chosen by her class, crowned the statue of Mary in church as the "Queen of Heaven and Earth." The whole school and parents attended the May Crowning.

One summer, five priests were ordained from our parish. Usually, two or three were ordained each summer. We witnessed their first Masses, often singing in the choir or serving at the Masses. At the time, no one thought this was particularly extraordinary. It was part of the tapestry of parish life, and inspired other young men to continue this tradition.

The total climate of "being Catholic" included the religious atmosphere in our homes, the commitment to the faith of our parents, and the multiple activities that were part of our everyday growing up as Catholics. These activities formed the spiritual climate within which we learned. This climate incorporated our Catholic beliefs and practices into a unified whole in Catholic parishes, with or without Catholic schools. This was far more important than how religion was taught. It formed the basis of our identity. In fact, the teaching of religion was secondary to the Catholic environment, or climate, in forming our commitment to the Church and telling us who we were as Catholics.

Catechetical instruction cannot be appreciated in these years unless one acknowledges the power and hold that the overall Catholic climate of the family, parish, and Catholic school had on children and adults. This needs to be taken into account when asking why many older Catholics are so faithful to the Church, and why many children, youth, and younger adults today lack commitment to the Church and her teachings. The Catholic climate made us who we were. This is no longer the case, and the results are obvious.

Secondary School

Transition into Catholic high school in 1948 was uneventful. Most boys in our parish went to Elder High School, a Catholic boy's school that we could walk to in ten minutes from St. Williams. The girls went to Seton High School, a Catholic girls' school, right across from Elder. Elder was named after Archbishop William Elder who was archbishop of Cincinnati around the time that the school started. Seton took the name of Saint Elizabeth Seton, the eighteenth-century foundress of the Sisters of Charity who staffed the school. The same Catholic identity that we witnessed in elementary school continued into high school.

Forty or so full-time diocesan priests taught at Elder, with only three laymen on the faculty. Our teachers were young and vibrant, eager to help us in whatever way they could. They played sports with us, took us to math and science fairs, attended our sporting activities, and moderated our clubs.

Elder's teachers were our friends, advisers, and role models. They played a major role in forming our emerging Catholic identity as we passed through adolescence. They inspired us to become good men, and encouraged a few of us to consider the priesthood. In my graduation class, eight seniors went to the diocesan seminary. On the other hand, this faculty, mostly made up of priests, also gave good training to the majority of the students who eventually married or remained single. The energy, dedication, and example of these good priests had a positive influence on us. We wanted to imitate them, regardless of what vocation we chose.

Something similar happened at Seton High School, a Catholic school for girls staffed by young Sisters of Charity. They also motivated the girls to become solid Catholic women. A few followed them into religious life.

Many of our classmates attended Mass every day in their parishes, before they left for the high school. On a given day, fifty-five high school boys and girls could be found at my parish, St. William's. We celebrated daily Mass, received Communion, and then walked to school, getting there about ten minutes before classes began.

Priests heard confessions daily at Elder and St. William's. Young men and women, struggling with their emerging adulthood, found consolation in this sacrament, especially as they dealt with their sexual development and the other issues that adolescents face.

As with Catholic elementary schools, the overall climate of Elder and Seton Catholic High Schools played a powerful role in developing our Catholic identity. This Catholic climate was more important than what we learned in religion classes. At Elder, we used the adult version of the *Baltimore Catechism (Vol. 3)*. It contained more sophisticated answers than we learned in the first two volumes of the catechism used in grade school. It also included biblical quotes.

In addition, we studied religion from a Catholic religion series in four volumes. It was entitled *Our Quest for Happiness*. Edited by Right Rev. Msgr. Clarence E. Elwell and written by numerous Catholic writers, it beautifully and precisely articulated the basic beliefs and practices of the Catholic faith. Ten or so years later, when I began my teaching career at Purcell Catholic High School, the series was still used.

Early Teaching

When I began to teach at Purcell High School, a Catholic boys' school, in 1960, most of my seminary classmates were also teaching in Catholic high schools. In a way, teaching was an escape from the close oversight of pastors in the parishes where we lived. In those years, much stricter rules existed for the young priests. Purcell provided a supportive community of diocesan and Marianist priests and brothers.

The Catholic identity of Purcell was similar to that of Elder. Students were imbued with Catholic ways in their homes, parishes, and grade schools. The inspiration of young priests and brothers teaching there was similar to that at Elder. Once more, this Catholic climate had a more powerful effect on the students than what we taught them in religion classes.

During my last year at Purcell in 1963, the upperclassmen seemed to be getting restless. This was the beginning of the turmoil of the 1960s. The turmoil was partially motivated by the emerging struggle for civil rights for African-Americans in the South. Student dissatisfaction with the religion books that we used reflected this uncertainty.

At this time, the changing secular and Catholic climate necessitated a change in catechetical delivery. Therefore, my religion classes began to focus more on key issues of the times — issues that the students faced. Less attention was given to the slavish following of the religion texts, chapter by chapter, question by question. The Catholic climate of the students was beginning to change. It was this generation of young people that a few years later became the progressives or radicals of the 1960s and 1970s.

In 1964, Archbishop Karl J. Alter of Cincinnati transferred me to teach religion and begin a counseling department at Marian High School, a Catholic girls' school. The subtle uncertainty about the teaching of religion experienced at Purcell intensified here. One symptom of a cultural shift was the hysteria and frenzy the girls displayed when The Beatles visited Cincinnati. The assassination of President John F. Kennedy in Dallas and the civil unrest and riots that developed later also suggested that the Church would need new ways to engage the culture and teach religion.

My spare time was occupied in writing a textbook for juniors at Marian High School and dealing with the morality of events and issues facing both teenagers and adults. Even at this time, students tended to be turned off by traditional ways of teaching religion. But somehow, my approach met with such success that, one day, Monsignor Carl Ryan, the superintendent for Catholic schools in Cincinnati, came into my class unannounced and sat there for the entire period. Later, he asked me to write a textbook series for the archdiocesan Catholic high schools. He wanted the texts to employ the approach I was using to teach the class he attended. Thanking him for the invitation, I politely declined his offer.

The uncertainty at Purcell and Marian High Schools portended revolutionary changes in the Catholic Church, Catholic schools, and Catholic faith formation. These changes came into full bloom during the latter years of Vatican II and afterward.

When this uncertainty spread, many Catholics maintained loyalty to their previous way of being Catholic. They questioned Vatican II reforms and maintained their traditional orientation within the Catholic climate.

Section 3:
SUMMARY OF MAIN TRENDS AND OBSERVATIONS

Here are ten key observations about the religious formation of children and adults before Vatican II.

1. The pre-Vatican II Church was a stable and well-organized society of Catholic believers.

In the United States, the Church existed as part of a much bigger cultural context, which, for the most part, was stable and regulated by rules of conduct. In the broader society, for example, civil law looked down on or forbade divorce and remarriage. Abortion was outlawed. The early years of the twentieth century were tough times, marked especially by the Great Depression and the two world wars. Movements for black equality and women's rights had not gained the momentum that would come in the second half of the century. Americans knew who they were and were proud of their identity.

The Catholic Church was stable and well-organized. Catholics did not question that their Church was the true Church, and that every other religion was flawed, some more than others. Little or no dialogue existed between Catholics and other religions, although each year, the Church prayed for the unity of Christians in the Church Unity Octave.

Every year, these days of prayer focused on bringing Christian denominations and other religions into unity with the Catholic faith. Catholics prayed that those outside of the Church might see their erroneous ways and unite under the pope, the Bishop of Rome. Ecumenism was practically nonexistent. In this environment, Catholics were convinced that they were right.

2. The Catholic Church was a relatively closed system.

In a closed system, the dynamic between the members is locked within the boundaries of the organization. A closed system is more or less impervious to outside pressures. Before Vatican II, the Church's relatively closed system served as a guardian of the culture in Irish, Polish, German, Maronite and other ethnic parishes. It was also the nexus for all religious, social, educational, and recreational activities in those communities.

Although Catholics lived and worked in the world, the Church's rules and requirements framed their psychic orientation and attitudes. For example, Catholics abstained from eating meat on Fridays. It was considered to be a serious sin to deliberately violate this law of the Church.

As a young priest teaching in high school, we often went to an outdoor hamburger restaurant with adults and students after Friday football or basketball games. We ordered from a speaker phone hanging on a pole where we parked. While I sat there in the driver's seat of a car, it wasn't unusual for students from Purcell or Marian High School to come to my car window. They would say: "Father, I forgot and ordered a hamburger and ate half of it. Can I finish it, or do I have to throw it away?"

These students lived in the world, but Catholic teaching guided their lives. Some of their Protestant friends laughed at them for asking me, but it didn't bother them. The relatively closed system of Catholicism dictated what they had to do in the world where they lived. Most Catholics lived this way and did not question Church teaching, even if they sometimes violated it.

In reviewing this manuscript, Sr. Marilyn Kerber, a member of the Sisters of Notre Dame de Namur, added some of her own insightful reflections on this period. She grew up in Chicago, and then entered her community, which had its motherhouse in Cincinnati. She became a Catholic school teacher, catechist, archdiocesan director of religious education in Cincinnati and president of the National Conference of Diocesan Directors of Religious Education. Speaking of her time in Chicago as a young woman, she said:

> The closed society accurately described here led to a certain defensiveness of Catholics. We believed that we had the true Church and were proud to be Catholic. As teenagers, we went to national rallies of the

Catholic Students Mission Crusade (CSMC) and proudly sang our rallying cry in school and elsewhere. It was a song entitled *An Army of Youth*, written by Daniel Lord, SJ.

Sr. Marilyn spoke energetically as she described going to a downtown hotel in Chicago for this youth rally. Cincinnati was the National headquarters for the CSMC. It was housed, appropriately, in a small building which was actually a real castle and was called "Crusade Castle". This organization remained very vibrant until the 1970s.

She continued telling of other activities that inspired Catholic young women. One in particular stuck in her mind. It was called "SDS," which stood for "Stop the Demand for the Supply." This Catholic movement stressed modest prom dresses. Members of the movement went into stores and demanded that the owners supply modest dresses for proms. If the stores refused, the girls would not buy their dresses there.

The Catholic climate also included Our Lady's Sodality for young women. The young women prayed the Rosary and were engaged in Catholic action. Teenage boys and girls could also join the Junior Legion of Mary. This group focused on saying the Rosary and distributing Catholic literature to barber shops, beauty shops, and doctors' offices.

These organizations and activities point to the pride that Catholic youth took in their faith and their commitment to it. This was part of a strong Catholic climate, shored up by the solid leadership of priests and religious. Obviously, there was also clear teaching of Catholic beliefs, and great devotion to the Mass and the Blessed Sacrament. Nonetheless, change was in the wind.

In the 1950s and early 1960s, seeds of unrest and portents of a changing future surfaced. An early indicator of this was the renewed appreciation of biblical scholarship and the critical study that followed in its wake. Initial unrest in the civil rights demonstrations and concern over books such as Teilhard de Chardin's *Phenomenon of Man* set the stage for the upheaval that erupted after the Second Vatican Council began in 1962. The former solid rock of Catholic belief and teaching was developing cracks. These broke open and unleashed a flood of emotions, energy, and doubt by the mid-sixties.

3. To appreciate religious education and Catholic identity during these years, it is more important to see the power of the Catholic climate than to concentrate on the teaching of basic Church doctrine.

The strong Catholic climate was taken for granted. Catholics accepted what the Church taught as true. There was no questioning of Church authority in regard to faith and morals. Matters of faith were clearly spelled out, and Catholics accepted them.

Catholic students learned the basics of their faith that they needed to be "good" Catholics. Teachers did not always concentrate on the nuances of right and wrong that might come up in real life. If difficult questions did come up, a Catholic could always ask a priest for the answers. Students learned what was necessary for a thought or action to be a mortal sin. They also had to know that committing a mortal sin meant that the act itself must be serious or grave — that is, killing someone unjustly or stealing a huge sum of money. Catholics also understood that a person must have given sufficient reflection and full consent of the will to the mortally sinful thought or doing the action. Particular situations often differed, but the fundamentals of the faith remained the same.

At that time, the peer pressure to live in unity with the Catholic climate and follow Catholic teaching and practice were powerful incentives. Children obeyed their parents and never questioned a priest or nun. Teenagers did not eat meat on Fridays, and if they forgot when out on a date or at a football game other Catholics reminded them. They never thought of missing Mass on Sundays. They were Catholic and did what Catholics did.

4. Religious education was effective because Catholics believed in and trusted the Church.

Great respect existed for the pope and bishops whom Catholics rarely or never saw, even on television. Bishops retained the vestiges of medieval monarchs and often lived in large mansions and had their own cooks and butlers. Bishops usually remained aloof from the people. These remnants of a bygone age were evident in their elaborate dress on official ecclesiastical occasions. The only time I saw a bishop in elementary school was when Bishop George Rehring confirmed me in the second grade.

Priests, to a lesser extent, received this same kind of respect from the people. What they said was considered as gospel truth. After all, they stood in the place of God. Priests were really involved in their parishioners' lives, thus promoting holy living and many religious vocations among both men and women.

Catholics believed that the Catholic Church was the one, true faith. It had all the answers to gain salvation, and Catholics had to follow the Church's teachings.

5. The Catholic family played a central role in faith growth.

Today, many Catholic couples do not teach their children the tenets of their faith or raise them as Catholic. Some are largely ignorant of what the Catholic Church teaches. Pre-Vatican II Catholics often knew little more than rote answers to questions about Catholic beliefs. They knew, however, what Catholics did and how they were to live. They prayed at home, had a great devotion to Mary, went to Mass every Sunday, abstained from meat on Fridays, and adults fasted during Lent. Catholics also respected priests and nuns, supported the Church, made sure their children learned about Jesus, and sent them to Catholic schools or religion classes.

The Catholic family was the most important factor in the faith development of the children. This faith development occurred not so much through what parents taught their children about Catholic beliefs, but by how they lived the faith every day. They celebrated Catholic rituals and were faithful at home to Catholic devotions, like the Rosary. Children learned from parental example who a Catholic is. Living faith is always stronger than "discussions" about faith.

Many Catholic parents had little formal religious training, since they often came from various ethnic cultures. Often, they knew little English. Nonetheless, they had one thing in common — they were Catholics. They found strength and comfort in their faith. They had great devotion to the Mass, the sacraments, and to Mary. They were committed to passing their faith on to their children.

When things began to change in the early 1960s, many parents did not understand why new means of teaching religious education to their children were suddenly being used. Up to this time, they trusted the priests and the nuns who taught in Catholic schools. Generally, Catholic parents went along with whatever "Father" or "Sister" did.

Things changed, however. Some parents became especially sensitive when sex education was introduced into the classrooms by some teachers. Many parents questioned whether or how sex education should be taught in classrooms. They often maintained that it was the prerogative of the parents. Parents challenged some books that religion teachers used. But the problem was that, often, sex education was not taught in the home at all. This was a sensitive area, and many parents strongly opposed teachers when they tried to teach it in Catholic schools.

6. Catholic identity was formed largely by the Catholic climate of the time.

The first five points of this section indicate the strength of the Catholic climate in rooting people's Catholic identity. Put simply, Catholics knew who they were, what they believed, and how they were to act in various circumstances. Identity is formed primarily by the ritual patterns that one learns and lives by. These included praying before and after meals, saying morning and evening prayers, reciting the Rosary, not eating meat on Fridays, and going to Mass every Sunday. Such ritual patterns formed the underpinning, largely unconscious, for the way that Catholics lived, believed, and acted. As long as these patterns remained solid and firm, the issue of Catholic identity did not surface. Before Vatican II, ritual patterns like these were clearly established for Catholics who were expected to live by them. Together, they formed the strong Catholic climate which helped shape Catholic identity.

Religious education's role was to teach Catholics what they were to believe, and how they were to act within and beyond the confines of the Catholic Church. After Vatican II, this Catholic climate weakened. Among other reasons, the questioning attitude inherent in secular culture became more prominent in the Catholic community. Catholic teachings were often questioned, and the Catholic practice of attending Mass, celebrating the sacraments, and praying shifted. With these changes came the gradual breakdown of what formed the groundwork for strong Catholic identity.

7. Organized adult faith formation sessions were rare.

Catholics commonly believed that by the time they finished the adult version of the *Baltimore Catechism III*, they had all the information they needed to live a full, Catholic, adult life.

This does not mean that Catholics never read religious periodicals, newspapers, or books. We got the *Catholic Telegraph* weekly in our home. Many Catholics subscribed to *Our Sunday Visitor* or *Maryknoll* magazine, which told stories of its missionaries.

Such Catholic publications kept Catholics informed. But, they focused primarily on information, not formation, even though learning about the faith was a mode of formation itself. Catholic faith formation happened largely through the collective influence of the Catholic climate itself, and through the Mass and sacraments. In fact, Catholics believed firmly that the basics of their faith could never change. This was symbolized by the Latin Mass that was the same wherever one traveled throughout the world. Catholics learned the basics of their faith from the catechism.

Before Vatican II, Catholics felt that if they had a good grasp of the teachings of the *Baltimore Catechism*, they had all they needed to live a full, Catholic lifestyle even in the secular world. Consequently, in this environment, adult faith formation played a limited role.

In saying this, however, we need to remember that there were movements to support faith formation. Among these were the Christian Family Movement, Catholic retreats for men and women, and the Catholic Students Mission Crusade. But, Bible study groups, continuing faith formation for adults, and similar movements only became common after Vatican II. At that time, the Church opened her doors to deeper communication with the secular world and to ecumenical dialogue.

Then, the Church encouraged Catholics to develop a mature adult faith, not one focused on Church rules and a defensive behind-the-walls mentality. That mindset had characterized Catholicism since the Protestant Reformation, and which the Council of Trent held in the sixteenth century.

8. The Church put little emphasis on biblical studies, except for defending the faith.

When my mother was a child, a Catholic nun told her that it was a sin to read the Bible. We never had a Bible in a prominent place in our home during my childhood. When I was in school, teachers never told me that it was a sin to read the Bible. But, they implied that I should be careful if I read it, because I might misinterpret its meaning.

Teachers told me to let the Church interpret the Bible for me, through Catholic teachings. They told me to accept the Church's interpretation of the Bible, as it is found in the *Balti-*

more Catechism, and in the sacramental system. Outside of its use at Mass and in the sacraments, the Church used the Bible largely as an apologetic tool to prove the Catholic Church was the one, true Church.

Bible study groups were rare in Catholic parishes. Protestants had these groups, but Catholics followed the teachings of the Church on Scripture. Only in the seminary was the Bible taken seriously. Even then, we never appreciated the wisdom that it contains. Later, we discovered this wisdom. We saw the vital role that the Bible and the Liturgy of the Hours play in the life of the Church, and in a Catholic's life.

Interestingly enough, the renewal of biblical scholarship was first set in motion by Pope Pius XII's encyclical *Divino Afflante Spiritu (Inspired by the Holy Spirit)* in 1943. It encouraged the translation of the Bible from the original texts, and eventually led the way to the renewal of Catholic biblical scholarship and textual criticism.

9. The teachings of the Church were God's Words, and Catholics learned "proofs" to show that Catholicism is correct.

The Church used Scripture to give arguments for the truth of Catholicism. Catholics did not doubt Church teachings which reflected God's divine will. We learned these teachings, often by memorizing the *Baltimore Catechism.*

In my second year of college at the seminary in 1954, the religion professor used Cardinal Pietro Gasparri's catechism which was written in Latin. We memorized three answers for three questions for each class. We had to be able to recite them back in class and for our examinations. Such education did not foster critical inquiry, but reiterated Church teaching. No one dared to question what was in this or any other catechism.

10. The Catholic climate was strong and stable and provided the underpinning for Catholic teaching and practice.

Catholics accepted this Catholic climate for what it was. They did not question it, assuming that it reflected divine teaching given by God. This remained true until Vatican II, when Catholics began questioning. When this happened, they questioned many teachings and practices of the Church.

The strong Catholic climate had been the most important factor in providing a foundation for teaching the Catholic faith. Everything that happened in these years was rooted in this climate. Before Vatican II, what was taught and how it was taught was not as important as the stable foundation that allowed for the ready acceptance of whatever the Church taught. When this strong Catholic climate began to shake and crack after Vatican II, everything changed. Even though the faith foundation of the Catholic faith remained rock solid, the Church was severely rocked by the tempests that swept over it.

The world and society were changing. Pope John XXIII's calling of a new Vatican council was a prophetic recognition that the Church needed renewal. The council brought to the forefront new ways of thinking and doing things, some of which already existed in the secular world and the broader Catholic culture. Pope John recognized the importance of bringing the Church into harmony with shifts that were occurring in the world. Through the wisdom of the Holy Spirit, the Church boldly accepted the new directions that emerged at the council. This resulted in profound changes and opportunities for the Church. They came about with much sacrifice and pain. As the results of the council appeared, Catholics were ill-prepared for the changes and began asking "Why?" This led to the breakdown of the strong Catholic climate and significantly affected the teaching of religion.

The Catholic climate described in Chapter 1 and its impact on religious education set the stage for what happened in the next decades. The strong and closed climate of Catholicism changed with new directions set by Vatican II and the cultural changes occurring outside of the Church.

CHAPTER 3

ECLECTIC – CHAOTIC PERIOD

(Late 1960s to 1980)

"Jesus never said, 'Go forth, arrange things.' No, He said, 'Go forth, I am with you.' This is our beauty and our force."

(Pope Francis. *Address to International Catechetical Congress*, September 27, 2013)

The time after Vatican II witnessed some of the most radical changes in the Church since the Protestant Reformation. The Reformation shook the Church to its foundations. At that time, the Council of Trent (1545-1563) responded to the Church's need for reform. This council set the stage for the life of the Church up to Vatican II.

The atomic bomb that exploded in Japan in 1945 hastened the end of World War II. Photos of the explosions in Hiroshima and Nagasaki show a massive mushroom cloud expanding in every direction, engulfing everything in its path. Gradually, the toxic particles in the cloud fell back to earth, spreading in ways unknown and unforeseen by its developers.

In a very different way, Vatican II (1962-1965) released a cultural explosion that rocked the Church and propelled it in new directions. The "fallout" spread far and wide, with many un-anticipated results. Unlike the atomic bomb, of course, the council was a work of the Holy Spirit and was called by Pope John XXIII to bring new life and hope to the Church and the world.

This period, from the late 1960s to the early 1980s is described in this book as the Eclectic – Chaotic period. The dates given for this period are somewhat arbitrary. They are based on changes in society, the Church, and my own personal experiences. During this era, catechesis floundered, but the Church's social ministry provided a beacon of hope. Positive catechetical renewal happened, but it was eclectic and sometimes chaotic.

The term "eclectic" describes the experimental and pragmatic aspect of secular culture, religious education, and liturgy. Society as a whole was changing. Church ministers tried to figure out how to adapt Vatican II teaching to the needs of Catholics. As the pre-Vatican II system broke down, latent energies inherent in the Catholic community burst into full Catholic awareness. With the questioning that ensued, religious educators abandoned the old ways of the *Baltimore Catechism,* which they then believed insufficient. What was to take their place? No one was quite sure. So, experimentation followed, and the Catholic climate became more ambiguous.

The term "chaotic" describes the confusion that existed in religious education and catechesis. Catechists wanted to know what to teach and how to teach it. In the pursuit of answers, Catholic university campuses became hotbeds for innovation, "fuzzy theology," and questionable conclusions. Many traditional professors in seminaries and universities were ignored by those caught up in the dynamism of change.

Often, these scholars retired or were eased out. The ideas of the catechetical innovators were soon disseminated on Catholic college campuses and in periodicals and journals. Then they were disseminated to the broader community of priests, catechists, and parents.

This chapter addresses catechesis during this period. It is divided into three sections. Section 1 considers the background of the times as it affected the Church and catechesis. Section 2 reflects on my own catechetical journey through these changing times. Section 3 summarizes the trends and conclusions described in Chapter 3.

Section 1:
HISTORICAL PERSPECTIVES

Catholics growing up immediately before this period could not have anticipated the radical changes in store for them. Children and adolescents of any era usually question many things. Before Vatican II, they questioned their parents and other adults. They questioned themselves as they grew through adolescence. They knew that they, like their parents and significant adults, could be wrong. When it came to the Church and Church teaching, however, there was a difference. We did not question the Church, but accepted her teachings as the Word of God.

The Catholic culture and climate planted in us the firm belief that the Church represents God, and that Church teaching reflected God's will. Consequently, we dared not question it. We feared God's punishment for disobeying God's laws and teachings. As children and young people, we accepted all the Church taught as God's divine will. This mindset was the same in adults. In my growing-up years, Catholics did not question the Church.

Setting the Tone

When the relatively closed Church opened up, the secular culture poured in. This set the tone for the environment that developed in the Church. There were currents of anger, rebellion, and freedom in society. Everything seemed up in the air, and almost anything seemed tolerable. The Church did not operate in a vacuum, and these changes affected every aspect of her life and ministry.

Social and cultural changes outside the Church shaped the way that Vatican II teachings were accepted and incorporated into Catholic life and practice. Fueled by unrest surrounding the Vietnam War, the civil rights movement, and the emergence of feminism, the U.S. culture was shifting and turbulent. To understand the direction that catechesis took after the council, one must see it within the framework of the times. Without appreciating the secular cultural environment of the 1960s and 1970s, it's difficult to appreciate the challenges that the Church faced during this period.

Changes in the larger culture filtered into the Church, and Church leaders reeled in the aftermath of the council. Bishops, priests, and nuns made strong efforts to choose the right direction among conflicting opinions. The laity often did not know what to do or believe. Many resisted the decisions to change the language of the Mass from Latin to the vernacular, to drop Friday abstinence and the Lenten fast, and to shift the holy days of obligation. They wondered, too, why Catholic devotions were downplayed and why the Rosary was de-emphasized in some areas.

A Catholic climate still existed, but it was different. It concomitantly exhibited energy, joy, fear, enthusiasm, concern, and wonder. No one knew quite how to respond, as parishes and catechists struggled to bring their parish liturgies in line with directives coming from the council.

Some Catholics enthusiastically embraced the new ways, many resisted, and still others didn't know what to do. The Catholic climate was ambiguous, resembling an amoeba in its fluidity and flexibility. Many priests, religious women, religious education directors, and parish catechists tried new ways to catechize. Others acted more like counselors and minimized catechetical teaching. Some priests resisted the changes in the vernacular and a small number made up Eucharistic prayers, so bizarre at times that I wondered if they celebrated a valid Mass. One even changed the words of consecration.

This environment upset more traditional Catholics who clamored for the old ways. Some bishops were so deluged with directives coming from Rome, from the U.S. bishops' conference, and their own dioceses that one wonders how they kept it all together. Diocesan religious education directors sometimes wondered how they would get through the day. They were under many pressures coming from all sectors. Many Catholics affirmed what was happening, but others complained about how religious education was being handled.

In this period, bishops, priests, nuns, and the laity embarked on various paths to renew the Church. Some abandoned traditional ways of prayer, including devotions and the Rosary. Others held on to the old ways and traditions. New methods of teaching religion and celebrating the liturgy brought fresh directions. Some Catholics wondered if everything was up for grabs, and if what they had learned as children was still valid.

The difference between Catholics and Protestants became blurred in the eyes of many Catholics. Experimental liturgies surfaced. Creating art collages and holding sensitivity sessions replaced content lessons in some religion classes. Traditional Catholics didn't know what to do. Often, they kept silent or insisted on the old Latin Mass and *Baltimore Catechism* teaching. Usually, their voices were drowned out or ignored.

Changing Catholic Attitudes

Secular attitudes affected Catholics on every level. As women increasingly took their place with men in the workplace, more pressures were exerted on families. Parents spent less time with their children and attention to children's sports intensified. These changing behavioral patterns affected "the domestic church," the home, and weakened the religious environment of the home.

Once, Catholics accepted the Church's teachings without question. Now, many questioned issues such as the ban on artificial birth control, but did not receive answers that satisfied them. The same applied to new teachings on the liturgy. The teachings may have been clear, but some Catholics simply did not accept them, and they looked elsewhere.

Aggressive, traditional voices intensified, demanding clear and accurate Church teachings on the parish and school levels. Catechist formation from the diocese and parishes often focused heavily on methods, with insufficient effort given to basic teachings. This did not satisfy traditional Catholics.

The 1970s were creative and exciting times. But, to call this period chaotic without acknowledging how much religious formation was also happening isn't fair or truthful. Much effort went into new catechetical directions, as was reflected in the Cincinnati Religious Education Assessment Program (REAP).

REAP documents were guidelines for directors of religious education, and for other diocesan programs. They gave directives on teaching basic beliefs and developing new methods to catechize. New catechetical materials proliferated, and effective teaching happened in many places. Bishops did their best to oversee what happened, and religious education offices produced admirable results.

During this time, media use in religious education took on new meaning. Films and filmstrips were commonly used as catechetical tools. When used properly, films were valuable in first Communion preparation, morality classes, and in other areas. Problems arose when they were used with no real attempt to also include solid catechetical instruction. Audiovisual resources set the stage for the explosion of other media influences later: the Internet, iPods, digital technology, and new media forms that are important tools for today's catechesis.

A Challenge to the Church

Signs of change in the Church, hinted at before Vatican II, were seen everywhere soon after the council. Catholics were encouraged to develop a mature faith, and many of them questioned their faith in this new era of freedom. With that, everything changed. The questioning process changed the face of Catholicism.

Children picked this up from their teachers and parents. It no longer sufficed for a teacher to present the Church's teachings and expect students to automatically accept them. Now, teachers had to relate Church teaching to those being catechized.

Erosion of Church authority intensified in 1968 with Pope Paul VI's publication of *Humanae Vitae* which has often been referred to as the birth-control encyclical. Many Catholics judged this beautifully written defense of human life by one small section that condemned all forms of artificial birth control.

In making his decision, Pope Paul VI went against the majority report of his own commission. It recommended loosening the Church's stance on artificial birth control. Instead, he followed the minority report of this commission which reaffirmed the Church's traditional condemnation of artificial birth control.

Reaction to *Humanae Vitae* was immediate, swift, dramatic, and widespread. Many theologians, clerics, professionals, and laity opposed the encyclical. Others accepted it, while still others were not sure. In one seminary, a professor put a public statement of opposition to it on the seminary wall. Similar things happened in other places. In commenting on this issue, a professional Church woman minister said, "I think that the role of women and their reaction to *Humanae Vitae* was an important factor leading to the decrease of Mass attendance and church participation." Then she continued, "Women, particularly mothers, are often the transmitters of the faith, and when they were disenfranchised by the church because of teachings and lack of recognition by the church, they failed to pass the faith on to their children."

The controversies surrounding *Humanae Vitae* rocked the faith of Catholics. The following comments typify the sentiments of some Catholics: "The Church said we can't practice birth control. We are forced to do so, for we can't bring children into the world and not care for them. We decided to practice birth control and still be Catholics. But from this time on, it is harder to accept Church authority."

Many sociologists claimed that this was the major issue that weakened the real authority of the Church in the minds and hearts of Catholics. The uproar over it continued for many years and accelerated the erosion of Church teaching authority. Its ramifications are still felt today.

The strong allegiance of many Catholic faithful to Church teaching, evident before Vatican II, vanished in less than ten years. Regardless of one's personal view on artificial birth control, the effect of it was devastating, as far as Church authority was concerned. It also had an undeniable impact on some mothers who were the key to passing on their faith to the children.

As I've explained, in the 1970s, the underlying Catholic climate was uncertainty. Many parishioners — traditional and progressive — were dissatisfied with the institutional Church. Some felt the Church was moving too slowly. At the other end of the spectrum were Catholics who believed that their Church had changed too much and was becoming too "Protestant." Still others felt that the Mass and Church teaching were outdated and did not speak to them, or to their children.

Such adult uncertainty produced negative effects on children. Many adults complained and questioned Church teachings at home. They attended Sunday Mass less frequently. Parental attitudes and actions negatively impacted their children more than anything else. Few realized the long-term consequences of the secular culture and such negative parental attitudes as children grew up.

In these years, there was a strong emphasis in the Church on religious liberty and conscience formation. Inadequately catechized, some Catholics picked and chose what they wanted to believe. Many rejected the Church's teaching on artificial contraception and were split on issues like the ordination of married men and the ordination of women.

Paradigms change when the former ways of doing things no longer suffice to meet the emerging demands of a new era. This certainly happened in catechesis, and must be taken into account when evaluating this period.

Experimentation and Innovation

Experimentation in religious education was manifested as college professors, religious educators, and catechists tried new ways to teach religion. This led to confusion in parents, students, and more traditional teachers. Some bewailed the fact that the *Baltimore Catechism* was no longer used, and that their children learned little about their faith. In fact, this experimentation sometimes went too far. One major religion textbook "rewrote" the Ten Commandments, using words and illustrations different from the traditional commandments. When a Catholic school teacher showed this to me, it became clear that something had to be done to curb the chaos.

Some Catholic university professors and other teachers denied essential truths of the faith. This included basic moral principles — even the divinity of Christ. Some parents who sent their children to Catholic colleges and universities for a Catholic education challenged college and university officials. They wanted to know how these institutions could be called Catholic. Some university and college teachers were called on the carpet by diocesan boards, as inquiries were made as to their orthodoxy.

On every level of Church life, innovation was common. Many religion teachers seemed to love experimenting. Some catechists replaced the memorization method with art exercises such as creating collages or watching films without stressing the basic beliefs that they contained. One religious educator, calling himself a catechist, was more interested in discussing student problems than teaching basic Church doctrine. While this happened, voices opposing liberalizing moments remained more or less silent. Their opposition was lost in the noisy enthusiasm for experimentation.

Confused parents did not know how to handle changes in the teaching of religion. Some bishops, immersed in other pressing Church issues, did little to oversee catechesis. In fact, they shifted this responsibility to their religious education offices. The old, stable climate of Catholicism had practically vanished.

Discussions on whether it was a mortal sin to deliberately miss Mass on Sundays without a good reason ensued. During this time, the Church dropped Friday abstinence, changed the rules regarding fasting during Lent, and shifted the number of holy days of obligation. The Church played down the Rosary, especially at Mass. It addressed sexual issues and changed the laws related to Catholics marrying non-Catholics. These issues intensified the ambiguity in adult Catholics. Meanwhile, Catholic youths and children picked up the uncertainty reflected in the wider Church.

Many wondered what it meant to be Catholic. If theologians, pastors, and Catholic adults didn't agree on matters of faith and morals, what should Catholics believe? What should catechists teach? With the focus on progressive trends in society and the Church, some religion classes were more like therapy sessions than catechetical classes teaching basic Catholic beliefs. Where this happened, it resulted in theologically illiterate Catholics. Catholics grew ignorant of what the Church believes, and what it means to be a Catholic. For some, being Catholic was associated with the Church's social teaching and the responsibility of Catholics to minister to the poor and needy. This, however, was not the full picture of what it meant to be a Catholic.

This ambiguous Catholic climate eroded Catholic identity as younger generations of children and youths grew up in uncertainty and turmoil. The Church's authority diminished. Children once heard their parents speak positively about priests, bishops, Church teachings, and social affairs. Now, they heard questions and complaints about them.

Young Catholics knew that some elementary and high school religion teachers, including priests and religious, disagreed with Church teachings. Their teaching sometimes blurred the distinction between the ordained ministry and the priesthood of the baptized. This led students to wonder what was true. Catholic children quietly internalized the uncertainty about the Catholic faith and what it taught. As they grew into youths and adults, the climate that they grew up in profoundly affected them, and many stopped going to church.

It is inaccurate, however, to say that during this period the teaching of the basics of the faith almost ceased. In going over newsletters from the Office of Religious Education in Cincinnati from 1973 to 1979, it became evident that much was offered on every level to assist catechists and catechetical leaders to teach the truths of the faith. Although this period is sometimes described as one of "paste and collages," these newsletters also reveal that great things were going on in some places to help further the faith. Among them were solid courses on catechesis and the teaching of the basics of the faith. These courses were offered to catechists, but not all catechists took advantage of what was offered. When catechists weren't well trained, those they were trying to catechize suffered.

In this confusing mix, catechesis was buzzing and alive. So was liturgy. While traditional parishes changed and focused on Mass in English, some free-floating parishes emerged. These parishes drew Catholics looking for alternative forms of worship. Some Catholics were dissatisfied with the slow pace of regular parish changes. They failed to realize that authentic change takes time. There was no easy fix when entrenched rituals, like the pre-Vatican II Mass rituals and sacramental celebrations were drastically changed or modified.

At some Masses celebrated in "free-floating" parishes, priests made up Eucharistic prayers or freely changed the wording. In these celebrations, a biblical reading was sometimes replaced by a secular one. The sign of peace lasted for an extended period, with much laughing and hugging. In one liturgy, the sign of peace was given more importance than receiving the Eucharist. In another place, those gathered put more effort into interpersonal dialogue than listening to the Word of God.

While this took place, serious-minded parents worried about the religious education of their children. Many teachers discarded the *Baltimore Catechism* in favor of students sharing with each other and making collages. In the early seventies, there was limited supervision over what basic teachings were taught in Catholic schools and in parish religious education programs. Bishops caught up in the pressure of the times weren't sure what to do. They tried different ways to hold things together, but most had limited success.

Parishes struggled to deal with changing views of parishioners, some wanting the "new" while others wished to hold on to the traditions of the past, including the Latin Mass. More conservative Catholic voices were set aside or bypassed. They were seen as old-fashioned and out of date. Such uncertainty and lack of solid teaching of the Catholic faith led to devastating consequences for generations. Many young Catholics grew up almost totally unaware of what the Church is, what it teaches, and what its rich history could teach them.

The tensions of the time distressed many priests, religious, and laypeople. Catholics took different sides on how to celebrate the liturgy or what to teach. Some priests and religious became caught up in the "liberated" spirit of the times and entered inappropriate relationships, fell in love and left religious life. Others, not wishing to cope with a new and complex Church or with personal issues, also left to live a married or single life in the world. A few bishops did the same.

Critical Times

The relationship between Catholic college professors and the bishops was a matter of much discussion. This influenced a memorandum, sent by Archbishop Joseph Bernardin of Cincinnati to the delegates of the Roman Synod on Catechesis. His memorandum, dated September 1, 1977, suggested what to include in the final document released to the United States. He discussed aspects of catechesis, stressed the needs of families, and focused on the need for solid religious formation. He also reflected on what he thought the relationship between bishops and Catholic college professors should be.

The archbishop appealed for unity in the Church and stressed the "complementary roles of bishops, theologians, and catechists." Toward the end of his statement, he said: "In today's catechetical scene, the theologians, because of their teaching positions in our colleges and universities, de facto, exercise more influence in teaching than the bishops. It is not a healthy situation, and every effort should be made to bridge the gap. If this happens, many other problems will take care of themselves" (Part One, 3).

When he returned from the synod, Archbishop Bernardin said that he appealed for this change on the floor of the synod hall. This indicates the influence on catechesis that university and college professors had in the years after Vatican II. It also demonstrates the difficulty bishops had in exercising their pastoral leadership in catechesis.

Lecturers spoke at national conferences in the 1970s and 1980s about ministry and catechesis. Notable among these events were the East Coast Conference, the Hofinger Conference in New Orleans, National Catholic Education Association Convention (NCEA), Ohio Catholic Educational Association (OCEA), National Conference of Diocesan Directors of Religious Education (NCDD), Los Angeles Religious Education Congress, and the Gathering in Chicago. These assemblies presented the latest and most innovative suggestions for religious education. Keynote addresses, lectures, and workshops highlighted the meetings. Textbook publishers, diocesan leaders, priests, and members of religious communities attended. Presentations were motivational, focusing on new ministerial and catechetical methods. These conferences influenced the development of catechesis from the 1970s to the end of the twentieth century.

The 1970s were critical times for catechesis. The paradigm shift occurring in catechesis in the aftermath of Vatican II provided the seeds for future consolidation and growth. While many catechetical experiments were questionable and seem superficial today, we can understand how and why they happened. Well-meaning religious educators struggled to do their best to address the changing needs of the Catholic community. They had been awakened by Vatican II, and immersed in the free — spirited secular movements of the day.

Solidifying Catechesis

Changes in the Church necessitated clarifications in religious education. In 1971, the Sacred Congregation for the Clergy published the *General Catechetical Directory*. Soon afterward, under the auspices of the National Conference of Catholic Bishops (NCCB), the U.S. bishops issued *To Teach as Jesus Did*. This document was soon well accepted by religious educators. It took a holistic approach, addressing adult formation, universities, schools, and catechesis itself. For several years, its stress on "message," "community," and "service" were the rallying call of religious educators.

Contrasted to this work, more traditional publications of the bishops, like *Basic Teachings for Catholic Religious Education*, issued by the NCCB in 1973, and to *Live in Christ Jesus* (1975), a pastoral reflection on the moral life, were not as impactful on religious educators. They were more concerned with new approaches to faith formation.

Soon after these publications, the U.S. bishops, following the directives of the *General Catechetical Directory*, initiated the most widespread catechetical consultation ever conducted in the Catholic Church in the United States. The goal was to write a national catechetical directory (NCD). The final form, entitled *Sharing the Light of Faith,* was released in 1977. The NCD became the official document that influenced catechetical developments in the United States for the next decade.

The input of traditional Catholics in the catechetical consultation phase of the NCD was extensive. Well-organized conservative Catholic groups asserted their beliefs and challenged more progressive Church movements. Their voices were a factor that dulled any future efforts at widespread consultation.

In 1975, Pope Paul VI published his apostolic exhortation *Evangelii Nuntiandi (On Evangelization in the Modern World),* a classic writing on Catholic evangelization. It was the foundation for the Church's future efforts in evangelization. Another significant work was Pope John Paul II's 1979 apostolic exhortation *Catechesi Tradendae (On Catechesis in Our Time).* It clarified many catechetical issues and laid the foundation for the *General Directory for Catechesis* that was published some years later.

Although other Church documents touched upon catechesis, the ones mentioned above were the most significant. They provided directions for religious formation in the latter part of the twentieth century. They also addressed the liberalizing trends that swept through universities, Catholic parishes, schools, and the Catholic population.

Sharing the Light of Faith, the National Catechetical Directory for Catholics in the United States (NCD), published in 1979, solidified catechesis in the United States. But it did not bring complete consensus about the best catechetical approach.

In preparation for *Sharing the Light of Faith,* Most Rev. John F. Whealon, archbishop of Hartford, sent a letter and questionnaire to all the bishops of the United States. In it, he asked, "What do we need, within the Catholic Church of the USA, to bring proper order and direction into catechesis?" (Letter to U.S. bishops, March 21, 1974). This question reflected the real need at this time, namely, reestablishing harmony and order in the catechetical enterprise. Eventually, *Sharing the Light of Faith* did much to accomplish this goal.

Catholic views on the state of catechetics were polarized. In contrast to the liberal tendencies widely present, Catholics United for the Faith strongly opposed new catechetical directions. They claimed that these new ways of doing catechesis minimized the teaching of the basic content of the faith. Members of this organization voiced strong opposition to more progressive directions in Catholic schools, parish schools of religion, and among professional catechetical leaders and directors of religious education. They challenged the catechetical community to maintain the orthodoxy of Catholic teaching during this chaotic time.

The *Wanderer,* a national Catholic weekly newspaper, supported such conservative voices, while the *National Catholic Reporter,* a more liberal weekly, covered the more progressive elements of the Church. In retrospect, both newspapers served the Church in presenting the two different faces of catechesis.

In summary, different models for teaching the content of the faith existed. The progressive ones focused on change and new ways. The traditional ones concentrated on basic Church teachings. Often, the traditional approaches were at the bottom of the list. Many times they were neglected by those with more dynamic ideas.

Priests and pastors had different views. Many enthusiastically adopted new ways of teaching religion, while others opposed them, preferring instead to stick with traditional ways. Often, parents and catechists did not know what to do. Many preferred the new ways, while others did not. Still others were confused and frustrated. Finally, not all bishops were in agreement. Some remained traditional, others moved in the opposite direction. Still others let the diocesan religious offices decide what to do.

The close-knit Catholic climate that prevailed prior to the 1960s broke apart with the shifting social fabric of America and the changes in the Church. Cultural changes outside the Church and new directions set by Vatican II changed the Catholic climate.

Looking Back

Reviewing this period, two additional things are worth mentioning. The first one pertains to the full-time position of CCD coordinators or parish directors of religious education (DREs). The DREs were the first real lay leaders in the Church after Vatican II. They were often responsible for more than just catechesis. Many moved out of Catholic school positions to assume this ministry. Later on, they often switched to other emerging parish ministries, like RCIA coordinator or pastoral associate. Eventually, many parishes and dioceses changed the title of their ministry position to "catechetical leader." These people were real pioneers in the field of lay ministry. Where well-prepared men and women were hired for this DRE ministry, positive results often occurred.

The second observation deals with priestly preparation. If priests had been better prepared to explain the changes taking place with parishioners after Vatican II, things might not have been as chaotic for the Church. Priests were not in agreement over many theological and pastoral issues. It was hard for them to discern the best way to address these issues. All of this intensified the uncertainty in the broader Church.

Section 2:
MY CATECHETICAL JOURNEY

In June of 1964, Archbishop Karl J. Alter of Cincinnati asked me to study for a PhD degree in philosophy at St. John's University in Jamaica, New York. He wanted me to prepare to teach at Mount St. Mary's Seminary in Cincinnati, Ohio. When I arrived at St. John's, it didn't take me long to realize that something was about to break loose in the English and philosophy departments. Tensions were high and the teachers were demanding change. Professors and students had strong but diverse convictions about human freedom and the changes sweeping the Church.

Winds of Change

The winds of change first blew across secular and Catholic college and university campuses in the 1960s. As a result, many Church changes were first spawned on university campuses as professors explored new ideas in seminars and classes. Progressive movements were refined within their walls. Even though St. John's was a traditional Catholic university, it was caught up in social changes sparked by civil rights issues and social protests. This uncertain political climate accentuated tensions surrounding religious changes initiated by Vatican II. By the fall of 1964, these tensions boiled over on campus. In particular, there were tensions over academic freedom and women's rights.

An American Association of University Professors (AAUP) chapter was formed there to support the rights of the professors. Initially, this union of faculty members was not recognized by the administration. From this group, however, new energy arose as the union put increasing pressure on the administration. Tensions entered the classrooms and spilled over into the hallways. Some professors seemed more committed to controversial issues than to teaching. At the end of my first year, one professor, deeply involved in the AAUP, forgot to give us a final examination.

Over Christmas break, the university fired about twenty professors, including tenured faculty involved in the union. Among the leaders of the protesting group was a priest. This led to a three-year strike at St. John's, the first university on the East Coast to experience a faculty strike. The strike mirrored what happened the year before at UCLA on the West Coast. The UCLA strike was a student-initiated strike; the St. John's strike was initiated by the faculty. It was paradoxical to see members of the Teamsters Union walk through faculty picket lines at St. John's. At the time, the Teamsters did not believe academics should unionize. This began a period of turmoil that lasted the entire time that I studied at St. John's for my PhD.

St. John's was not unique. Energy for change swept through many colleges and universities. Lectures on the new changes in the Church and the theology behind them were held there. Fordham University took a leading role in presenting lectures discussing what happened at Vatican II.

On Catholic college campuses and in dioceses, renowned professors from around the world and delegates from the Second Vatican Council lectured on Vatican II changes. They addressed thousands of students, professors, and interested

Catholics. In the audiences, there were also Protestants, and elementary and high school teachers, including many priests and nuns.

This exciting and energizing time brought positive and negative developments to the Church. In some places, Church teaching became the object of scrutiny, questioning, and sometimes rejection. Catholic elementary and secondary teachers brought home what they learned at the universities and taught it to young and old alike. As this happened, the questioning and the uncertainty of ordinary Catholics grew.

By the time my graduate work was completed in the spring of 1967, unrest was widespread. A week before taking up residence as a professor at Mount St. Mary's Seminary of the West in Cincinnati, the rector was changed and the seminary was suddenly in turmoil. Students openly challenged seminary rules, demanding change. Eventually, Archbishop Alter addressed the students and confronted the faculty, wanting to know what was going on. When I returned from St. John's in May 1967, the seminary felt more like a morgue to me than a lively academic institution. The tension continued there into the 1970s. Many changes that took place were student initiated.

Widespread protests occurred in Catholic and secular universities and colleges around the country. Some students tried to take over the president's office at the University of Dayton, and professors were called on the carpet by Church officials for their questionable teaching in matters of the faith.

The riots in Chicago during the 1968 Democratic National Convention spoke loudly of the angry climate of the country. Unrest spread elsewhere, and activists demanded freedom, as did rebellious guitar players and "pot" smokers. The clothes that hippies wore manifested this rebellious attitude. Woodstock, the 1969 outdoor rock-music festival, became the symbol of free expression in this era.

The cry for freedom was also evident in seminaries. Some seminarians wore scraggly beards down to their waists, as well as Afro haircuts and old, torn jeans. Those who were later ordained looked back in humor or embarrassment when they see their youthful pictures from seminary days. Today, they are amazed at the differences between the seminarians of the 1960s and 1970s and today's seminarians.

Behind this unrest loomed the Vietnam War, in which thousands of American men and women gave their lives. It was a highly unpopular war and led indirectly to the intensification of the civil unrest and the tragedy at Kent State University. At Kent State in 1970, Ohio National Guardsmen killed four protesting students and wounded many others.

Clarifying Issues: *Religious Education Today*

In the early 1970s, concern grew among parents and in parishes over the state of religious education. At that time, I was teaching philosophy at Mount St. Mary's Seminary of the West in Cincinnati. My residence was at Our Lord Christ the King Parish. After several fledgling parish directors of religious education asked for my help, I became involved in religious education at that parish and wrote a three-part series of articles on this subject. I then sent them to the diocesan paper, the *Catholic Telegraph.*

Cincinnati Archbishop Paul Leibold put my articles together in a pamphlet and sent them to the parishes of the archdiocese. He called the pamphlet *Religious Education Today*. It

described the state of religious education. It also told the story
of religious education up to the 1980s. It began by saying:

> The efforts of professional religious educators dur-
> ing the past few years have not succeeded in lessen-
> ing the acute problems facing the Catholic Church
> in the Christian training of youth. With the shifting
> emphasis of Vatican II and the putting aside of the
> *Baltimore Catechism* as the chief vehicle of Catholic
> instruction, about ten years ago, educators started to
> reexamine the methods of teaching religion. (p. 1)

Describing catechetical innovations, it stated that the "first
efforts stressed Salvation History, and centered on the Bible as
the history of God's dealings with his people" (p. 1). Then, it
added that this approach was not generally successful because
it placed too little attention on the mental and psychological
attitude of the students. They often said that it did not speak to
their needs. About the same time, another catechetical initiative concentrated heavily on social concerns almost as if "religion should be equated with race relations or working in the
inner city" (p. 1). This approach also proved inadequate.

Next, the catechetical focus shifted to the interpersonal,
stressing love, relevance, and commitment. My booklet reported, "Some religion classes became little more than elementary psychology classes, with little psychology and less religion
taught" (p. 1). Finally, in the early 1970s, it added, "many
religious educators emphasize making religion a good experience for children" (p. 1). In addition, these educators often told
teachers to stop being so concerned with children and concentrate more on adult education.

Concerning teachers, *Religious Education Today* stated that the uncertain condition of how and what to teach made it difficult for teachers "to present the basic teachings of Catholicism. They, themselves, are often unsure of what has changed and what remains the same" (p. 1). Referring again to teachers, the pamphlet said: "They are rapidly coming to the conclusion that if they are to continue calling their education 'Catholic,' they better start teaching youth what the Catholic Church is all about. How this can be done is a crucial question at present" (p. 1).

Religious Education Today described two main trends. The first was reflected in the catechism method, while the second stressed interpersonalism and human experience. From that time on, the relationship between what is taught and how to teach it has been a major issue. The pamphlet went on to point out"

> The catechism emphasizes the teachings of the Catholic Church. Religious educators today criticize this method as lacking the dynamism needed to bring fundamental Catholic beliefs within the experience of the learner. They remind us that often in the past, people never moved beyond their grade school catechism analysis of religion. They seldom questioned, and if they did, felt guilty about it. Many failed to appreciate that faith should grow as people do. (p. 2)

Religious Education Today mentioned that failures of this method are found among adults. It stated: "Because of the uncertainties in the Church some are questioning their faith. The rigor of their early training makes it difficult for them to accept what has happened during the past few years. They are threatened, finding the secure faith of yesteryear gone. No longer is the Church a safe haven. Some become defensive, other stop going to church" (p. 2).

Then, it said that the catechism method presenting Church teaching had been so certain, so authoritarian. Catholics were taught what to say when they prayed, how to answer objections against the Church, and how to distinguish between mortal and venial sin. They were given guidelines for the overall governing of their lives. It continued, "Religious educators are the first to point out that neither life nor the teachings of Christ are as cut and dried as the Church had claimed prior to Vatican II" (pp. 2-3).

Many Catholics made up their minds about what to believe and how to act around the time that *Humanae Vitae* was released. As this happened, many priests, brothers, and sisters left religious life. This had a strong impact on the teaching of religion to children, teenagers, and adults. Lay Catholics were looking for more than they received from the catechism of the past. *Religious Education Today* explained:

> The result was playing down of the catechism by teachers and religious educators, almost to the point of mockery. It was no longer looked upon with respectability. (p. 3)

Then, the pamphlet continues:

> Today religious educators are taking another look at the main thrust of the catechism, namely to teach the basic truths of the Catholic faith. Emphasis on 'content' is coming to the fore once again. The problem is how to incorporate the post-Vatican II teachings

of the Church within a dynamic, person-centered framework. (p. 3)

The remainder of the pamphlet stressed both experience and content. "The second factor that the proponents of the experience-centered approach minimize is factual information or content" (p. 4). It continued, "The latter is essential for any human experience, for man's response depends upon the facts he knows.... Hence, to say that children should not be taught facts about their faith and other religions does not make good psychological sense."

Religious Education Today concluded:

An ideal solution for religious education would take the best elements from both the catechism and the experience-centered approaches. These are an emphasis on factual content, within the dynamic structure of lived experience. (p. 5)

The hierarchy made numerous efforts to address the issues raised in *Religious Education Today* as the erosion in catechetics continued throughout the late 1960s and into the 1970s. Through their teachings and writings, they continued to reiterate the basic truths that came down from Jesus to bring stability to religious education. Their pleas often went unheeded as widespread experimentation seemed to be never-ending in religious education and catechesis.

Changes in society and the Church affected all segments of Church life, especially religious education. I was thrust into the heart of these changes when I was sent away for doctoral studies. The pressure on me intensified when I became director of religious education in Cincinnati in 1973.

Accepting the Invitation

My formal journey into religious education began in the summer of 1973 when Archbishop Joseph Bernardin of Cincinnati called me while I was on vacation in Nevada. The call surprised me, and I wondered what he wanted. He asked me to visit him after my vacation to discuss getting into religious education. This call put a damper on the rest of my vacation, for I knew that religious education was in great turmoil. My basic instincts told me to have nothing to do with it.

My experience with some parishes that were reluctant to change, my consulting with catechetical pioneers in the local parish, and the pamphlet I'd written may have given the archbishop the wrong impression. He may have assumed that my interests were in religious education and that I knew a lot about it. The opposite was true.

The archdiocese had recently held diocesan synod in 1971, before I received the archbishop's call. It put diocesan religious education under the leadership of the Catholic School Office. It allowed one slot for a religious education consultant for all the parishes.

I was convinced that model would not work. So, anticipating my meeting with Archbishop Bernardin brought me much anxiety. When he asked me about assuming the diocesan religious education position, I hesitated. He told me that I was to be responsible to the school office personnel. Before answering him, I reflected and then gently said: "Thank you, but I am not your man. I am happy to keep teaching philosophy at the seminary."

The archbishop seemed stunned at my response. He paused for a minute and then replied: "Bob, I'll never assign you to do this under your promise of obedience to me. But, I'd like to know what I can do to convince you to take this job." I was equally stunned at his openness.

I realized that I knew little about the field and that I would have to start from scratch. I knew immediately that I would have to hire a staff, and begin a new office. Since I was ignorant about hiring, budgets, and the management of an organization, I naively blurted out: "We'll have to start a new religious education office. I know hardly anything about budgets and management. So, I'll want to be able to spend whatever I need and have no other boss but you for one year."

At that, the archbishop thought for a minute, and replied: "I can't do that, Bob. We recently finished a diocesan synod which put religious education under the Catholic School Office. Besides, we need to have budgets and lines of responsibility." After explaining why I mentioned each item, he answered, "Let me think about it over the weekend, and I'll let you know on Monday."

On Monday, he called and said: "Bob, I will go along with your conditions. We'll have to work closely together to get this off the ground." Never expecting this answer, I answered: "Can I have a few days to consider it? I'll call you by Friday." He said, "Fine."

After that call, I left the rectory where I resided and spent three days in an old mobile home on my land in Indiana. There, I prayed for wisdom and walked the land. On the third day, I sat at the edge of a recently constructed pond and looked at the lakeshore. There, all kinds of water bugs scurried around, moving wildly on the surface of the lake. When I saw them acting in this erratic way, I thought to myself: "This is just like the craziness that I'll be dealing with in Cincinnati. I might as well go home and take the job." I packed up, returned home, and told the archbishop that I would be happy to accept his offer.

Up to the time of Vatican II, religious education in Catholic schools was taught chiefly by consecrated religious women. Students attending public schools learned their faith in Confraternity of Christian Doctrine (CCD) classes that were usually held once a week. CCD programs existed in almost all Catholic parishes. Sometimes, sisters teaching in the Catholic school handled them; in other places, the assistant pastor taught these classes. Few were handled by laypeople.

After Vatican II, parishes shifted focus. Some dropped CCD classes in favor of other approaches to the teaching of religion to our youth. For several years before Archbishop Bernardin asked me to take charge of religious education in the diocese, parish religious education was more or less unorganized. Tensions existed in the parishes. Many people wondered what could be done to establish new directions for religious education.

The archbishop hoped my appointment would tone down this diocesan unrest. Before I took the position, there had been three other people who had been selected for the job. The third one was sent away for several years to get a doctoral degree in religious education. The month before he was to begin his work in our archdiocese, he told the archbishop that he was leaving and moving to another city.

The Parish Directors of Religious Education Association (the DREs of the archdiocese) had planned a religious education convention for about 500 people. It was scheduled to take place two weeks after I had met with the archbishop. The DREs were a strong group and the only real voices of religious education in the diocese. Some had threatened to unionize if something did not change.

The archbishop was to address this convention and introduce the new religious education director of the archdiocese. After the person previously assigned for the position left, Archbishop Bernardin was stuck. He had promised the DREs a new leader and, for a while, he had none. Until I agreed to take the job, he was concerned about the reaction of this association. All of this background was unknown to me when he initially invited me into religious education.

My subsequent experience with Archbishop Bernardin began a great friendship. It lasted until he died in Chicago in 1996. At the same time, it thrust me into the center of controversies in religious education that lasted during my whole tenure as director of religious education.

Facing the Challenge

My entrance into catechesis was a baptism by fire. As I had requested, the Office of Religious Education was separated from the Catholic School Office. It was given responsibility for all religious education, including the teaching of religion in Catholic schools. So, some members of the school office staff became members of the religious education office. Tensions existed between the offices and in the parishes as religious educators and school personnel worked out their budgets and responsibilities.

Gradually, we hired new personnel. The office began to focus on religious education for all sectors of the diocese. As this happened, differences in parishes and Catholic schools over the teaching of religion led some to resist help from "downtown." On my second day on the job, a Catholic school principal called me. The first thing she said was, "Congratulations on getting the new position." The second sentence was, "Stay out of my school." A similar attitude existed in many parishes. Some of our staff members were often disillusioned when few catechists showed up for formation sessions. After a while, this changed. Parishes later saw that the Office of Religious Education provided significant help.

As the years went on, parishes and Catholic schools appreciated the work of the office and responded willingly. They welcomed our offers to teach courses, and we invited capable parish religious education directors and Catholic school religion teachers to help us.

Nonetheless, there was a small group of Catholics who aggressively wanted to return to the old ways of the *Baltimore Catechism*. These people accused staff members of teaching false doctrine. The pressures got so intense that Archbishop Bernardin finally had to intervene. He wrote a letter, addressed to Bishop Daniel E. Pilarczyk, Vicar for Education, to me as director of religious education, to Rev. Jerome A. Schaeper, Superintendent of Schools, and to all staff members of the education office. He wrote to respond to some articles about the Archdiocese of Cincinnati that appeared in the *Wanderer*. In his letter, he gave the Office of Religious Education his unconditional support. His comments appeared in the April 1975 edition of the religious education newsletter. The letter began:

During the past few months, I know that you and the members of your staff have been publicly and unfairly criticized. I regret very much that this has occurred. The purpose of this letter is simply to assure you and your associates that you have my personal support and that I am very grateful for your dedicated work.

In the final paragraph of the letter, he wrote:

I know from my personal experience that you and your staff have the dedication and competence needed to fulfill the important responsibility which is yours. I look forward to working with you in the months and years ahead.

This letter from the archbishop testified to how difficult these years were. Some staff members were verbally attacked. Others were accused of heresy, and we were secretly taped on several occasions by those searching for some area to challenge. Many challenges centered on sex education and teachings on moral matters. Other complaints were directed against how the Church's doctrinal content was presented. Still others were directed against parishes and Catholic high schools, where Catholic teachers were accused of heresy, and also against Catholic colleges and universities. Some charges had merit, but most did not. One religious community of women was unfairly described in print as being "chocked full of nuts."

In another letter, written to me on September 9, 1977, Archbishop Bernardin expressed his thanks for our support "relative to the picketing" that he experienced on "the occasion of the covenant between Nativity and All Saints parishes." In the letter, he mentioned that the picketers were from a traditionalist Catholic movement. No matter how hard he or anyone else tried to improve religious education and teach orthodox Catholic doctrine, it could not satisfy some Catholics.

It seemed that sex education was a particular sore point for many Catholic parents. In some instances, those criticizing materials used in some Catholic schools had reason to do so. But, for the most part, the subject was discretely and effectively addressed in schools. The problem, however, often came down to the unwillingness of those opposed to sex education to discuss the matter and to compromise. When addressing the legitimate criticism of a book about sexual matters used in some Catholic high schools, Archbishop Bernardin referred to the documents, *Human Life in Our Day* and *Humanae Vitae*. He tackled dissention over birth control and conscience formation by pointing to Church teaching on these matters. The archbishop said:

> It would be permissible in a text such as this [the text that was problematic] to indicate that there has been public dissent. It would also be possible to talk about how an individual might resolve the problem if, in good conscience, he cannot accept the Church's teaching in this instance. But this is quite different from giving the impression that the opinion of the dissenters has the same standing as the teaching of the Holy Father. (*Memorandum from Archbishop Bernardin*, February 4, 1974)

This memorandum reflects the climate of the times. Today, the question of dissent would not be permissible in any Catholic book used in faith formation programs. These were the issues, however, that had to be faced by Church leaders during this period. There was conflict from the right and from the left, and it was hard to get anyone to compromise. Archbishop Bernardin's love for God's people led him to try over and over to reconcile differences and bring peace.

Such an environment made staff members and parish catechetical leaders cautious. But, as dedicated Catholics, they knew that Jesus and His apostles had been attacked before them. The Church of the twenty-first century owes a debt of gratitude to such pioneering leaders in religious education. Without their efforts, the Church today would not be where it is.

Catechesis amidst Chaos

The newsletters published by the Office of Religious Education during the 1970s reveal much about religious education during this period. Many courses, workshops, and institutes provided content and methodological suggestions for parents, elementary and secondary school catechists, and adult faith formation programs. Published five times yearly, these newsletters were twenty-four to thirty pages long. Besides a myriad of catechetical courses for teachers of children and youths, the office offered extensive programs for business people throughout the city. Well attended and appreciated, these programs constituted only one small creative effort to catechize adults in the 1970s.

A lecture series on the Holy Spirit at Regina and Seton High Schools drew a thousand people at some sessions. Multiple courses, offered at Catholic colleges and universities were offered in cooperation with the Office of Religious Education. The same was true of courses in youth catechesis and youth ministry in Catholic schools and parishes. During this period, the Office of Religious Education staff conducted hundreds of workshops and sessions in parishes, schools, and other places.

In those years, professional religious educators and pastors put strong emphasis on adult religious education, now called adult faith formation. This was influenced by the growing popularity of the Rite of Christian Initiation of Adults (RCIA). It was believed that if adults were well informed about their faith, it would be easier for them to form their children in the faith.

Many multi-talented people served in the Office of Religious Education during these years. Reflecting on their accomplishments in the Ohio cities of Cincinnati, Dayton, Sidney, and elsewhere, it became eminently clear that many Catholics of that era did not leave the Church because they had few opportunities to learn and know the basics of their faith. Something more profound was occurring. The requirements of the Religious Education Assessment Program for teaching the truths of the Catholic faith give further testimony to this. The courses of study for the Religious Education Assessment Program and the archdiocesan school office illustrate in detail the specific items or protocols to be taught by religious educators and catechists in Catholic schools and parishes.

Many opportunities existed for parish and Catholic school religion teachers and parents to learn and then teach the basics of the faith. Diocesan requirements for catechists and catechetical certification were developed and approved by Archbishop Bernardin. These were consistent with teaching solid Catholic doctrine. The same thing happened in other dioceses throughout the country.

Some of these norms and requirements were not adequately implemented on a parish or classroom level. Dioceses could establish standards, but they couldn't force people to follow them. Parish and school catechetical leaders had to see to their implementation. Those with their own agenda, and those who did not follow solid guidelines from the diocese, usually accomplished little in the catechesis of children, youths, and adults.

Solid Achievement: Religious Education Assessment Program (REAP)

In 1974, the Office of Religious Education staff initiated a program for separated and divorced Catholics, brought the Christ Renews His Parish program into the diocese, and began a diocesan-wide catechetical process called the Religious Education Assessment Program (REAP). Fr. John Cavanaugh, the archdiocesan chancellor, directed it. He was a well-organized, non-threatening, and popular man. His supervision gave the program credibility.

REAP emerged from the work of many different committees. Committees on curriculum for elementary and secondary religion teachers and committees on certification requirements for catechists and catechetical leaders were among them. Other committees worked on the ministry of the catechist, directives for adult faith formation, and other aspects of religious education.

To ensure that the curriculum to be adapted included traditional basic teachings of the Church, a member of Catholics United for the Faith (CUF) was invited to serve on the REAP Committee. CUF was an unofficial watchdog committed to maintaining Catholic orthodoxy in religious teaching. This caused quite a stir among other committee members. But, it assured us that the final product would be well balanced and would include the traditional side.

REAP was an all-encompassing catechetical initiative. As it was developed, the staff offered many workshops for catechetical leaders and catechists through the diocese. In a period of ten years, many accomplishments came out of the Cincinnati Religious Education Office and from catechetical offices in other dioceses.

Complaints made today that Catholics received no solid catechetical teaching during these years aren't necessarily valid. REAP and the religious education newsletters of the Archdiocese of Cincinnati paint a different picture. Everything was not chaotic. Much solid teaching occurred. The reason why some Catholics left the Church and learned little about their faith is not as simple as saying that students were not taught Catholic doctrine. Sometimes this was true, but the reasons for Catholics leaving were far more complex, including the impact of secular society and the fractured and changing Catholic climate.

To get a better picture of catechesis in the 1970s, we consider two addresses, given on March 24, 1977, by Bishop Daniel E. Pilarczyk, Vicar for Education, and me. We were speaking at the Directors of Religious Education Assembly at Mount Notre Dame High School in Cincinnati. The topic was the REAP documents.

These addresses were later published in a pamphlet. We described the development of the ministry of catechesis during this era. In his address, Bishop Pilarczyk offered a vision of what religious education would be like in 2002, twenty-five years later. It is interesting to analyze what he said then, and reflect on what has happened since that time. He began:

> In the past fifteen years or so, religious education has been going through a kind of reactionary swing. Previous to that time, the emphasis had been almost ex-

clusively on content, or knowledge. Then the theoreticians began to remind us that experience has an important role to play in our religious development, and scholars began to announce that not all our knowledge was as firmly grounded as we thought. Religious educators responded to all this. Some would say they over responded, others that they over-reacted, and still others that the baby was thrown out with the bath water.

Perhaps the epitome of this period was the mythical religious educator who announced to the class: "There was no Noah, there was no ark, there was no flood, and so much for the content. Now let's all take out our crayons and draw pictures of how we feel about God." By now I think we are working our way out of that period of transition and turmoil in the confrontation between content and experience…. We need both the labor of the heart and the toil of the mind. We have reached, or are on the point of reaching, a kind of synthesis. (p. 9)

Then, the bishop said: "In our own diocese we are in the process of clarifying whom we want teaching and what we want them to teach. I am referring to the REAP guidelines on personnel and curriculum."

Here, we have Bishop Pilarczyk's estimation of the state of religious education in 1977, and in the tumultuous decades immediately before it. Let it be noted that, in his view, the period going forward would bring a synthesis of content and experience. In retrospect, Bishop Pilarczyk's remarks are one more indication that to blame catechesis almost exclusively for what subsequently happened in the defections of Catholics from the Church is a misreading of the times. The real reason must focus on the loss of the strong Catholic climate.

In spite of what was accomplished, the number of Catholics leaving the Church grew. Something more was happening here, and religious education was not the main culprit.

At the same assembly, my remarks focused on catechesis as an important ministry. I explained that catechists were responsible for serving the broader Church, calling forth the gifts of the community, and working together as members of the Body of Christ. My talk began with my hopes for the future. I explained:

> I see REAP challenging local communities to call forth the gifts present there. It urges more parish responsibility to recognize and develop leadership, especially in the area of catechesis. It involves a particular challenge to ordained ministers, as well as to principals and directors of religious education.

These words hinted at another challenge that catechesis faced — namely, the proliferation of new ministries. Church leaders often concentrated more on new and emerging ministries than on catechesis. Many dedicated Catholics, once committed to catechesis, moved away from religious education into new forms of ministry that they saw as more interesting and exciting. As this happened, the catechetical enterprise suffered.

Parishes and Catholic Schools

Clearly, tensions existed throughout the diocese and the broader Church pertaining to religious education. Differences of opinion were present within diocesan organizations. Turf issues surfaced between the religious education and Catholic schools offices. These differences often came down to who was in charge of religious education in the schools and how well the religious education and school office staffs related to each other. In Cincinnati, on paper, the Office of Religious Education was in charge of religion in Catholic schools and the parish director of religious education was in charge of teaching religion in the parish Catholic school. In reality, this was not always the case. In some parishes the ambiguity of who was in charge still persists.

This is illustrated by the following episode. The religious education staff announced the new diocesan policies for religion teachers in Catholic elementary schools at a Catholic school principals meeting in 1975. These policies included procedures for reporting the qualifications of each religion teacher in the elementary schools. After the meeting, two Catholic school principals looked me up in the back of the auditorium. Angrily, they said: "The only organization to whom we will provide information on the qualifications of our teachers is the State of Ohio. You will get no report from us." This episode symbolizes one of the many challenges that religious education faced.

Some school principles insisted that they, not the parish directors of religious education, were in charge of religion in the school. Such disagreements often had to be settled by the pastor, or by diocesan policies. Another issue surfaced over who had oversight for catechesis in the Rite of Christian Initiation of Adults (RCIA). How were catechists and catechetical leaders supposed to relate to those directing the liturgical aspects of the RCIA?

Differences existed between religious education and liturgy personnel on both the diocesan and parish levels. These

centered on staffing, finances, and who was in charge of liturgical catechesis in the Mass and sacraments. Diocesan religious
education offices across the country experienced similar tensions as those felt in Cincinnati. Funding for staff personnel
and money for needed programs were major issues brought up
at diocesan conferences and national assemblies. In addition
to children's and youth catechesis, adult faith formation often
developed according to the spirit of the Rite of Christian Initiation of Adults.

Lay Pastoral Ministry Program

This trying time required much patience. Yet, from the midst
of such turmoil, the seeds of something solid emerged. During my first several years in the Office of Religious Education,
I began the Lay Pastoral Ministry Program (LPMP) for the
archdiocese. It was a combined effort of the religious education office and the Athenaeum of Ohio, a Catholic seminary
in Cincinnati. The idea for this program first came on a picnic
with two former students. These women were recent gradu-
ates of Mount St. Joseph College and wished to dedicate themselves to some area of Church ministry. As they explained to
me, there was no university or academic program in the area
that admitted women into a graduate theology program that
focused on ministry.

After a long discussion, some interested friends were invited to discuss this matter two weeks later at Holy Family rectory
on a Sunday evening. I lived there at the time. To my surprise,
twenty-four people showed up. They all expressed interest in
some sort of graduate ministry program.

I spoke to Archbishop Bernardin about it the following week. He responded favorably, saying, "Bob, if twenty-four people are interested in a ministry program, this must be the work of the Holy Spirit. We have to follow up on it. Go see Fr. Ray Favret, the rector of Mt. St. Mary's Seminary, and the two of you can work out where it takes us." This began a process which led to beginning the LPMP program at the Athenaeum.

The theological initiative for lay ministry had roots in Vatican II. The council encouraged lay participation in the Church, and called the laity to work in the vineyard of the Lord. The fact that the Lay Pastoral Ministry Program came out of an initiative of the Office of Religious Education in 1975 might surprise some today. But, considering the climate of the time, it was not unusual. Offices were not organized as they are today. Greater flexibility existed in meeting diocesan pastoral needs.

Catholic religious and laity were hungry to learn and be part of the new and emerging Church. Ministry formation, broader than religious education, was at the top of the list of popular programs. Often, parish catechists preferred engagement in pastoral ministries to fulfilling catechetical responsibilities. Sometimes, this happened to the detriment of catechesis.

Section 3:
TRENDS AND CONCLUSIONS

In retrospect, we can ask, "What were the underlying causes of the erosion of Church authority and the changing Catholic climate after Vatican II?" No simple answer exists, but the changes relate to changing Catholic ritual patterns that shifted in the strong Catholic climate existing before Vatican II.

We can better appreciate this by recalling a basic principle of human communication: "If you want to upset a person or group, upset their rituals." The changes in the Mass upset Catholics. Dropping Friday abstinence and not requiring Catholics to fast during Lent also affected them. Why? Because the ritual patterns changed, and such ritual patterns were the organizational framework within which faith had previously been lived out.

Pre-Vatican II ritual patterns were solid and consistent. They expressed a certain way of doing things or a way of celebrating a mystery of faith, like the Mass. It was all part of the collective unconscious of Catholics. Take the Mass. Latin was the language used to celebrate this mystery of Christ's sacrifice on the cross and His continued presence among us in the Eucharist. All Catholics throughout the world worshiped this way. Friday abstinence from meat was the same throughout the world. These practices never changed. Through them, Catholics showed their unity as Catholics. Wherever Catholics went, the Latin Mass and Friday abstinence were the same.

Then, suddenly these strong Catholic rituals of faith changed, and Catholics wondered why. Their spiritual ritual life was turned on its head; so too was their Catholic identity.

Something similar occurred when the Lenten fasting requirements changed. When Vatican II changed these rituals, these traditional signs of what it meant to be a Catholic changed. When the old rituals changed, it affected the hearts of Catholics. First, they asked, "Why?" Then, they thought: "If these strong signs of what it means to be a Catholic can change, what else can change? What does it mean to be Catholic?"

In retrospect, such questions could have been addressed more effectively if adequate preparation had been given to

Catholics as to why the changes occurred. One reviewer of this book said: "Failure to prepare Catholics well for these changes rests at the feet of the priests and bishops. Unfortunately, many clergy were not prepared, and they failed to instruct their people. Where this happened, Catholics went out on their own or followed grudgingly."

Where good preparation happened, many parishioners saw the positive nature of the shifts in Catholic worship and Church teaching and loved them. This brought an exuberant new spirit to Catholics eager to link their faith to the changing culture of the times. The changes promoted by Vatican II bore fruit. Among them were an emphasis on the role of the Catholic in the modern world, liturgical renewal, the focus on religious liberty, the ecumenical movement, and the recognition that every Christian shares in the priesthood of Jesus Christ.

Nonetheless, as Catholics questioned, the strong Catholic climate changed. The relatively closed society that once was the Catholic Church ended. Such questioning was a normal reaction to such traumatic changes. In changing its ritual patterns and shifting its theological orientation, the Church weakened the underpinning of the Catholic climate which once was rock solid.

This change of ritual patterns was a fundamental cause of the eroding confidence in the Church, and the lessening of the authority of the Catholic hierarchy. As the rituals changed, Catholics wondered what else would change, or what was true in the changing world where they lived.

The spirit of Vatican II and *Dignitatis Humanae* (*Of the Dignity of the Human Person),* the Declaration on Religious Freedom, affirmed the need to form mature adult Catholics. This meant shaping one's conscience after due reflection and prayer. Catholics now thought for themselves, and began to take exception to certain tenets of the Church.

In summary, the Catholic climate that once kept Catholics united and was the foundation for religious instruction, broke down and eroded. As this happened, new directions had to be set.

We also remember the significance of cultural changes during this period. World events, coupled with post-Vatican II Church renewal, greatly impacted Catholics in the 1970s. This chapter focused on the uncertainties, ambiguity, and unrest that shifted the Catholic climate. The late seventies set the stage for what was to come, as catechesis moved in a more solid direction.

To appreciate what happened in the 1980s, we have to consider major influences operating in catechesis in the 1970s. They included the following.

1. Catholics shifted their attention from Church allegiance to what was going on in the secular world.

The Vatican II documents *Pastoral Constitution on the Church in the Modern World* and the *Declaration on Religious Freedom* emphasized the Christian's responsibility to enter into dialogue with the secular world. Many Catholics responded to that challenge. Notable among the issues that some Catholics embraced with vigor were the Vietnam War, the civil rights movement, the appeal for married priests, and the feminist movement. These issues brought heated discussions among Catholics with sharply differing opinions.

Regardless of what side Catholics took on religious issues, most embraced their opinions with vigor. They didn't always agree with official Church teaching. When dealing with heated sex education and textbook issues in the 1970s, I wondered if being diocesan director of religious education was more about "putting out fires" than setting the foundations for solid catechesis. Many Catholics clung to traditional Church teaching. Others were more concerned with finding something new in liturgy or religious teaching. When Catholics stopped taking Church teaching as the gospel truth and began to decide religious issues for themselves, the relatively closed Catholic community existing before the council crumbled.

When the full impact of the social and cultural changes operative in the 1970s came crashing down on the Church, Catholics were ill-prepared to handle them. Bishops found it difficult to exercise meaningful control over what was taught.

2. Many Catholics remained Catholic, but what it meant to be a Catholic varied greatly.

The Catholic understanding of what it meant to be Catholic depended on whether Catholics were social activists, religious conservatives, or institutional figures. As adults probed new issues, young Catholics of grade school and high school age suffered the consequences of a highly volatile, secular society. They grew up without clearly established rituals, patterns, or teachings that were the basis of Catholic identity.

Some young Catholics dropped out of the Church when they became adults. Those who remained were largely unaware of the core truths of Catholicism. They, in turn, taught their children very little. Gradually, age-old Catholic traditions disappeared from the lives of active and nominal Catholics. Young Catholics could no longer give a clear and convincing description of their Catholic beliefs and practices, including the Mass and sacraments. Catholic devotions, such as the Rosary, were not as common. Changes in Catholic worship caused more confusion in Catholic life until new forms were adopted. They significantly impacted the convictions that Catholics had before Vatican II about the veracity of their Church.

3. Religious women and priests also experienced many changes.

Many nuns, whose religious habits covered their whole bodies except the face and hands, changed to lay clothes. It was sad to see some of these women in their sixties and seventies attempting to dress in secular clothes. Occasionally, one saw a nun wearing a dress that had been in fashion thirty or forty years earlier, when she entered religious life.

Many religious women left their traditional convents and lived alone, or with other nuns in apartments. Others went further, saying, "If we live and dress like the laity, why don't we just leave, get dispensed from our vows, live the life of women in the world, and perhaps get married." Before religious women chose to dress in secular clothes, their identity was often associated with the habits they wore. When they abandoned traditional habits for secular clothes, this identity was challenged.

Religious women increasingly left the convent. Some couldn't cope with the changing dynamics in the Church. Others sought professional therapy to adjust to the changing times. What happened in religious communities is symptomatic of the challenges to the wider Catholic climate in the 1970s and later.

The religious women who remained took up the challenges of Vatican II. They became, perhaps, the most educated and most professional group of religious women that ever existed in the Catholic Church. They entered all sectors of society. Some remained as teachers. Others embraced the struggle for social justice. Still others moved to the top of religious and secular organizations as competent managers, administrators, and coun-selors. In a short period of less than forty years, religious wom-en transformed themselves. Following directives from Rome to return to the original charisms of their founders or foundresses, they made a profound impact on the Church and the world.

The ministry of priests also shifted focus. Their identity crisis arose when this shift took place. This happened as the laity increasingly got involved in parish ministry, formerly the exclusive domain of priests. Before Vatican II, priests cat-echized, kept parish financial records, made all decisions, and did everything at Mass except serve. With increased lay in-volvement in Church affairs, many priests asked, "What is my role as a priest?" "What is my identity?" This caused real unrest and priestly loss of confidence. I especially noticed this as I gave workshops and retreats to priests. At one point, I was not comfortable dealing with such dynamics in groups of priests. I declined invitations to address them for nearly ten years.

Some priests and nuns had entered religious life or the seminary as young as fourteen years of age. Suddenly, they found themselves as religious dealing with men and women in the secular world. This, along with more communication with each other, brought new temptations and challenges, including sexual ones. How to cope with their sexuality in an open soci-ety became a pressing issue. Many left, including those who fell in love. As priests left, some Catholics who received the sacra-ments from them wondered if the baptisms, confessions, and marriages performed by these priests were valid.

Such issues affected the greater Catholic population, chal-lenged effective catechesis, and weakened the fiber of faith formation as laypeople shifted some of their respect for priests and nuns.

4. A major paradigm shift occurred in the Church, and the results were typical of any major paradigm shift.

A paradigm is a master model. It attempts to clarify the underlying dynamics that operate on a preconscious level and keeps a community or group oriented in a particular way. The pre-Vatican II Church paradigm did this for many years. When things changed, the Church had to face the dynamics operating when a major paradigm shifts.

Paradigms exist in any group or organization. All disciplines employ certain ways of thinking and acting. For instance, until the late Middle Ages, the scientific world was governed by the paradigm described in the teachings of the ancient astronomer Ptolemy.

This paradigm presented the earth as the center of the universe, and based its astronomical calculations upon this fact. Christianity used this paradigm to teach that the earth was the center of the universe. Theologians and bishops of the time taught that Jesus came to the earth because it is the center of the universe. As the center, God sent Him here to redeem the whole universe.

When this paradigm was shown to be false by Copernicus, Galileo, and Newton, new ways of thinking were required. This shifted not only astronomical calculations but also required the Church to adjust her teaching. This proved to be painful and devastating to those who accepted the new theory that the earth was not the center of the universe. Many suffered or were put to death by the Inquisition for being "heretics."

When a major paradigm shift occurs, some enthusiastically accept the new. Others resist it, clinging to the old. During this period of change, as witnessed over and over in science, much uncertainty and experimentation exists.

Vatican II brought about a major paradigm shift in the Catholic community. When this happened, the underlying dynamics that once held the proponents of the old paradigm in faithful allegiance changed. As the new paradigm took shape, pain and uncertainty occurred as they always do when a paradigm shifts.

The 1970s saw the impact of energies released by Vatican II. Major changes in the ritual patterns of how Catholics acted and celebrated their faith were significant. This was especially evident in the changes of the Mass, the sacraments, fasting, abstinence from meat, the dropping of Rogation Days, and the changes in the traditional prayer life of Catholics.

Just as in science and businesses where significant changes in management and approach take place, changes in the Church produced uncertainty, unrest, loss of identity, and the other characteristics seen during any major paradigm shift.

A key challenge at the time of any paradigm shift involves decisions about how to teach and what to teach in the new paradigm. Within the Church, people wondered what should be retained from the old Church paradigm. They asked themselves: "What is so essential to Catholicism that without it authentic Catholicism ceases? What can change? What can never change?"

From the perspective of paradigm shifts, what happened in catechesis in the 1970s is understandable, although it was not anticipated in the Catholic community. Some historians claim that the bishops of Vatican II did not realize the full consequences of the council decrees. Regardless of one's view in this matter, many Catholics believe that the guiding hand of the Holy Spirit led the Church to make these changes.

Nonetheless, the Holy Spirit's presence in the Church did not guarantee that everything taught after Vatican II was accurate and correct. Many mistakes were made. In the midst of the changes, no effective criteria existed to judge orthodoxy or orthopraxis. Bishops tried, but they had limited success.

The 1970s witnessed the weakening of the bishops' authority. The tragedy of this was often beyond their control. It intensified in the 1980s and beyond because of the priest sexual abuse scandal involving some priests in the Church and how it was handled by the bishops. In the United States, the bishops' actions in addressing this scandal greatly affected the continuing erosion of their moral authority.

5. When the Catholic climate eroded or shifted focus, so did Catholic identity.

Prior to Vatican II, the strong Catholic climate, assimilated as part of their lives by most Catholics, provided a stable psychological foundation for Catholic identity. When the changes occurred, this Catholic climate gradually eroded. Along with it, the strong identity focus of Catholics disappeared.

When the questioning process after Vatican II intensified, the stable beliefs and practices of former Catholic ways changed. Among these were Friday abstinence from meat, Sunday Mass attendance, the Mass celebrated in Latin, devotion to the Rosary, and fasting during Lent. As these changed, Catholics searched for a new Catholic identity.

In their search, they received limited assistance from the Church, which was caught up in her own problems. Church leaders endeavored to sift out Catholic beliefs and liturgical practices in the aftermath of Vatican II. Coupled with this, issues arose in religious life, especially among vowed religious, as they rediscovered their original charisms and ventured out on new paths. At the same time, the priest scandal rocked the Church to its depths.

This search for Catholic identity continues today and involves more than the basic teachings of the Church. Identity is formed primarily through Catholic ritual patterns which changed in the aftermath of the council. As this happened, Catholic identity became unclear. With this ambiguity, the development of Catholic identity for some Catholics became more of an individual than a collective thing. Catholics could no longer rely on the Catholic climate to underpin their identity. The firm ties that once held Catholics together in a community had disappeared.

6. The breakdown of Catholic allegiance to Church teaching and practice accelerated.

Negative reactions to *Humanae Vitae*, Pope Paul VI's encyclical on human life, created the first crack in the solid wall of the Catholic faithful who had previously accepted and followed all the Church's teachings. The encyclical, which banned the use of artificial birth control, was widely opposed. Eventually, this encyclical led many to a "pick and choose" mentality concerning moral matters. While this happened, these opposing voices were countered by Catholics who insisted on traditional Catholic teachings and ways of doing things. Even priests and bishops did not always agree with the Church's teaching, and these disagreements became public.

Controversies about the morality of artificial birth control highlighted other conflicts simultaneously taking place. Many Catholics began using artificial birth control methods while continuing to receive the sacraments. Premarital sex was also a hot topic. Erosion of Catholic beliefs about other moral teachings of the Church continued as well. Among these teachings was the very serious issue of abortion.

Before this time, the question often asked of priests was, "Is it a sin to kiss?" Now, this shifted to, "Is it wrong to have sex before marriage if you really love the other person?" Divorce became more common, and civil laws that formerly outlawed divorce gave way to easy divorce. In 1973, abortion was legalized in all fifty states.

Such issues had a profound effect on catechesis. In some classrooms, students questioned Church teachings or engaged in heated debates on controversial topics which the teachers did not or could not resolve. Some priests and nuns questioned traditional Church teaching in many matters. But, most bishops, priests, and many Catholic laypeople continued to adhere to basic Church views.

Some reactionary groups tape-recorded lectures and workshops at local and national meetings, looking to discover theological "errors." It was distressing to speak at such meetings and know that every word had to be weighed carefully. No one wanted to be accused of heresy or serious theological mistakes. At the Los Angeles Religious Education Congress, speakers discussed among themselves a magazine published by a traditional Catholic group that was passed out as the people entered to attend the congress. The magazine urged the attendees not to attend certain lectures. Some angry speakers said that if their names appeared in the magazine, they'd charge more to speak the following year. This confrontational attitude added fuel to the fire, and more people attended these sessions than otherwise.

Most dioceses and national organizations became increasingly careful about whom they invited to address catechists and teachers. This was wise. Without such screening, different points of view, some contrary to Church teaching, surfaced. That left attendees more uncertain as they returned home. In spite of such efforts, confusion continued through the 1970s.

7. The first non-clerics well-educated in theology and catechesis were religious women but were soon followed by laypeople.

The professionalism and expertise of religious women challenged some priests. Then, as the laity became better steeped in Catholic theology, some people in the pews knew more updated theology than the priests.

A witness to the increasing education of the laity could be seen in the first class of the Lay Pastoral Ministry Program (LPMP) which I began in Cincinnati in 1974. Most students in the class were laypeople. After nearly forty years, this program is still thriving. It has graduated hundreds of well-educated lay ministers. The quality of ministry in Cincinnati today has been strongly influenced by the laity's response to the Lord's call to become educated and serve His Church. At the same time that the LPMP began, the diocese began admitting the first permanent deacon candidates.

In the 1970s, women's voices intensified, asking for more equal treatment with men in the Church. This centered on appeals for women's ordination, but was not restricted to that issue. These voices were inflamed by the publication of the Vatican document *On the Question of the Admission of Women to the Ministerial Priesthood.* It was published by the Congregation of the Doctrine of the Faith in 1976. In it, the Church made it very clear that women could not be ordained. The groundswell for women's equality that happened in the 1980s was initiated during this period.

8. Weekly Mass attendance changed little, but the seeds for a radical drop in Church attendance were sown.

Family structure weakened as Catholics became immersed in the secular world that swirled around them. For some, this included long business trips, meetings, and attendance at the activities of their children. When both parents worked, this required that one or both parents be absent from their family, and this brought added challenges to family life.

Eroding morality within secular culture shifted the sexual mores of some Catholics. Obscene television programs and pornography weakened the moral fiber of young and old alike. The increasing strength of the feminist movement changed the outlook of many people concerning women's rights and responsibilities. The need to exhibit "political correctness" became stronger. Advances in medicine brought new challenges, including moral questions about certain medical procedures. Such issues affected the Church in multiple ways, some healthy, others not so healthy.

Religious education was not immune from the challenges brought about by massive attitudinal shifts resulting from such changes. They came upon the Catholic community all at once, leaving unanswered questions: "How should catechists respond in teaching the faith? What should be said about women's ordination, married priests, and inclusive language?" Addressing such issues was difficult for anyone directly involved in catechesis. Catechists and parents alike searched for the truth and what it meant to be a faithful Catholic.

9. Changes in the Church set the stage for effective future catechesis.

In the 1970s, religious educators tried different approaches to catechesis and liturgy. Along with them, new ways of catechesis began to emerge. These took different forms and focused on teaching children and adults the basic truths of the Church and a love of Scripture. These approaches emphasized the importance of connecting what is taught with the experience and lives of those being catechized. In this regard, the catechist is challenged to inspire the catechized to reflect on what is taught in light of the present and the future, and to help them integrate what they learn into what they do, say, and think. Finally, the catechist is to help the catechized recognize the need to learn the basic truths of the faith, internalize them, and act accordingly.

In the 1970s, effective catechesis emphasized the central mystery of the Christian life — namely, Jesus' Paschal Mystery. He gave His life for us and was raised up by the Father. This is renewed at every Mass. Catechesis needs to teach the meaning of the Mass, its importance, and the need to celebrate it, and to regularly praise God and receive the graces necessary to live a solid, Christian life.

During the 1970s, Pope Paul VI and Pope John Paul II set the groundwork for future catechesis through their teachings and writings. They stressed priestly and ministerial formation. Following their lead, as this decade came to a close, Catholic theologians, priests, religious, and lay catechists began focusing more on the essentials of the faith. This continued into the 1980s. By then, the growing necessity of restating basic Catholic beliefs was clear. By the mid-eighties, the writing of the *Catechism of the Catholic Church* was underway. It would be published in 1994. After Vatican II, it took catechists several generations to discover new and effective ways to share Jesus' Good News.

CHAPTER 4

EXPERIENTIAL – SYSTEMATIC PERIOD

(1980s to 1990s)

> "Catechesis is a pillar for education in the faith and it needs good catechists.... Beginning with Christ means not being afraid to "go with Christ to the peripheries."
>
> (Pope Francis, *Address to International Catechetical Congress*, September 27, 2013)

The Catholic climate continued to flounder, and catechetical leaders continued to search for effective ways to catechize during this period. Experimentation declined and more intentional efforts were developed to effectively teach the basics of the faith. In this Experiential – Systematic Period, many catechists began inductively with lived experience, but searched for a systematic approach to teach basic Church beliefs.

As catechetical efforts were challenged from many quarters, new pastoral ministries took hold in the Church. Their increase impacted the commitment of pastors and pastoral leaders to catechesis. In the 1980s, enthusiasm for new pastoral ministries grew in the Catholic population. It was manifested by the variety of ministries that developed in parishes and were treated in workshops and at lectures at catechetical conferences.

Former catechetical leaders shifted their allegiance to other ministerial fields like social justice, parish administration, and youth ministry. New commitment to them masked the unresolved problems that catechesis faced when this explosion of ministries occurred.

To address the changing dynamics of this period, Chapter 4 is divided into three sections. Section 1 considers the history of this time. Section 2 reflects on my catechetical journey, and Section 3 summarizes the catechetical trends described more fully in this chapter.

Section 1:
HISTORICAL PERSPECTIVES

The secularization of culture had slowly intensified from the mid-1970s on. Seldom did religious leaders step back and recognize how profoundly it affected the Catholic population. It influenced the Catholic way of thinking and acting, and catechists and religious leaders struggled with this reality from then on. With materialistic incentives all around them, why should young people be interested in learning what their faith teaches? Why would they want to attend Mass which they often didn't understand? If it did not connect to their world, they stopped going. "Why should I go to Mass?" they asked. "My parents don't go very often." Secularity became the backdrop against which catechesis was interpreted.

The ambiguity in the Church, described in the first chapters of this book, began to subside. Yet, it continued to rear its head in catechesis and in the growing disregard of Catholics for Church teaching, especially that on birth control. Respect for

Church authority declined as a result of the bishops' handling of birth-control issues, women's issues, and clergy abuse cases.

The feminist movement grew in intensity. Women increasingly took their place alongside men in the workplace, often assuming positions of leadership. The feminization of culture influenced some Catholic women's attitudes toward the Church. They failed to see opportunities for women at the highest level of Church life. These feminist voices increased in intensity and challenged the all-male hierarchy to bring the Church in line with the twentieth century.

These and other factors led to the gradual erosion of Catholic confidence. Before long, Sunday Mass attendance dropped to under 30 percent. Prior to Vatican II, it had been as high as 90 percent. As Catholic worship patterns shifted, many left the Church, went to Mass only occasionally, or joined Protestant churches, especially evangelical churches. Some Catholics dropped out of Church involvement completely.

The catechetical enterprise continued to be powerfully impacted by secular culture. Relativism, secularism, and amorality intensified, especially with the introduction of the Internet. It provided a way to disseminate anti-religious and amoral information and material, especially pornography, nudity, and violence. Regular television programs also promoted the questionable conduct of entertainment and media heroes.

What was once considered scandalous dress for adults and teenagers became common. Even children's and infants' clothing began to mimic what adults wore. It was progressively more difficult for parents to monitor what children watched on television and what they viewed on the Internet. With pressure put on them to make more money to afford upscale lifestyles, fewer parents had the time to nurture their children and monitor the TV they were watching.

Divorce became common, and abortions increased, as did the use of birth control. Promiscuous behavior also increased. What was once considered the lifestyle of the hippie generation was no longer "off limits." It gradually filtered into the general population. This included drug abuse and sexual immorality.

The Catholic climate, once the strong bulwark of U.S. Catholicism, changed significantly. Catholics were "all over the ballpark" as far as their beliefs and practices were concerned. With a rapidly changing, secular world and inadequate catechesis in schools and parish schools of religion, two generations of Catholics emerged who knew little about what it meant to be Catholic.

As this happened, new catechetical documents appeared from Rome and from the U.S. bishops. These documents aimed at reinvigorating catechesis and liturgy. While catechetically sound, they did little to address the root problems, including the challenge of secular culture and the erosion of the Catholic climate. Even though Pope John Paul II was personally popular, his popularity did not significantly move the larger Catholic population to grow in respect for Church authority as a whole. Hierarchical authority influenced the average Catholic less and less. Catechists and liturgists searched for fresh ways to give interested Catholics solid Catholic teaching and ways to keep youths in the Church.

Catechetical Methods

Catechists could not stem the tide of Catholic erosion. Bishops, pastors, directors of religious education, and catechists recognized the importance of bringing order and direction to catechesis. New directions were needed, and there was little interest in returning to the *Baltimore Catechism*, although some traditional parents and teachers pushed for it. In the 1980s, the Archdiocese of Cincinnati developed ministry guidelines for catechetical leaders, as did many other dioceses. At the same time, an organization of parish religious education leaders called CREA (Cincinnati Religious Education Association) was initiated under the leadership of the archdiocesan Office of Religious Education. A similar organization, called DREA, began in Dayton, Ohio. Other dioceses established similar organizations. These groups provided support and assistance for catechetical leaders in their ministry.

Catechists tried new catechetical methods, and the role of the parish religious education director grew in importance. Although more ordered approaches to catechesis were put in place, free-floating catechetical sessions continued in some places. These sessions emphasized drawing, creating collages, and similar activities. Parish leaders and diocesan religious education offices emphasized catechist formation. Next to parents, catechists played the most important role in conveying the truths of the faith to Catholics of every age. While the dynamics of how to catechize and what to teach began to clarify, solid guidelines were needed.

Religious educators often focused on human experience as a starting point for catechists. The older, deductive method of the *Baltimore Catechism* gave way to new approaches. Thomas H. Groome was in the forefront of a movement that encouraged the sharing of human experiences. His book *Christian Religious Education*, published in 1980, had a significant impact on religious education. According to Groome, the catechist begins with human experience and invites the participants to share their experiences in a particular area or topic. This sets the stage for introducing the Christian message or content of faith in light of it. This inductive mode of learning attempted to connect experience with basic Catholic beliefs.

Attempting to follow this approach, some catechists focused too much on human experience and neglected the basics of the faith. Where this happened the catechized did not receive a complete and systematic knowledge of the faith.

Stressing the connection between the content of the faith and human experience was important. It led to new insights about how Scripture and Church teachings impact life and can challenge a person to live the faith more fully.

My catechetical approach began with Scripture and the message of faith, and then to apply it to the past, present, and future experiences of the catechized. This stressed basic beliefs. When God's Word and experience are connected, people are often led to a personal faith response. This also results in the internalization of God's Word, and to having new insights about what God's Word means in a person's life. The final stage is for the person to respond to the new insights gained through service to others, and through the celebration of faith in the sacraments.

By the 1980s, most dioceses had graded courses of studies for catechesis. These were standards for the teaching of content and for the use of suitable catechetical methods. These courses of studies contained specific content to be taught. The assertion that little content was taught in these years is quite unfounded.

Once courses of studies were in place, dioceses could evaluate the religion textbooks. Some texts they approved, but others they did not. Once more, this illustrates that religious educators expended considerable efforts during this time to provide catechetical content to students. In spite of such efforts, the faith of Catholic children, youths, and adults continued to weaken.

Even in stable, committed Catholic families, the faith of some members often wavered. It was progressively more difficult to get children to attend religion classes and to go to Mass. It was clear that the future stability of Catholics would rest largely on the Catholic home environment and on family faith formation. The Catholic climate continued to erode.

Emerging Ministries Challenge Catechesis

From a historical perspective, various forms of ministry increased in popularity. The title of my first book, the *Ministry Explosion* (1977), reflects what was happening in the 1980s. The explosion of interest in ministry did not help to revitalize catechesis. While catechesis floundered, other ministries began to flourish. By the end of the second millennium, many talented catechetical leaders moved from catechesis into the new, emerging ministries.

As new ministries developed, the challenge existed to clarify the meaning of the term "ministry." The second challenge followed the first. It pertained to parish revitalization in light of new, emerging lay ministries.

Meaning of Ministry

Prior to Vatican II, Catholics did not use the word "ministry." "Minister" and "ministry" were considered to be Protestant terms. According to the Protestant understanding, ordained and unordained Protestants exercised different forms of ministry. Catholics used a different vocabulary. Ordained Catholic men were called "priests"; Protestant pastors were called "ministers." Likewise, lay Catholics did "apostolic works"; lay Protestants did "ministry."

When Catholic priests, religious, and lay leaders began attending theological conferences and ecumenical gatherings after Vatican II, they picked up on the term "ministry." They began using it in a broad sense to refer to work done by Christians in response to their baptismal calling. Others reserved the term "minister" to refer only to those working in some official way for the Church — catechists, liturgists, Catholic school teachers, etc.

In the larger Catholic community, the use of "ministry" was soon picked up by Catholics who were searching for a deeper understanding of their baptismal calling. At first, many Catholic leaders, including bishops, used the term to indicate any ministerial activity coming from a person's baptismal commitment. So, some people talked about "the ministry of the laity." "Ministry in the marketplace" and "ministry in the family" were also discussed.

As the term became more generally used, many bishops proposed that the term should be used more narrowly and precisely. This meant a change to a more institutional focus on the word "ministry." That excluded the use of the terms for Christian work like "ministry in the marketplace" and "ministry in the family." This more restrictive use was eventually adapted by the National Conference of Catholic Bishops (NCCB) after extensive discussion in the early 1980s.

Before the term "ministry" was formalized, a reflection paper was published by the U.S. bishops (NCCB). The paper, "Called and Gifted: The American Catholic Laity," was approved on November 13, 1980, by the whole body of U.S. bishops. It used the term "ministry" in a wider sense. Under the heading of ministry, the document stated, "Baptism and confirmation empower all Christians to share in some form of ministry." Then, it went on to say that service in the world is sometimes called "ministry of the laity" to balance with the concept of ministry found in "ecclesial ministerial services." This reflection of the bishops also mentioned the notion of "family ministry."

Almost immediately after this paper's publication, the USCC's Theological Committee recommended that the term "ministry" be restricted to officially designated Church ministries, while the term "service" was to be used to describe forms of Christian work that follow the Gospel mandate. This recommendation was later accepted by the U.S. bishops as the official guideline for terminology to be used in all subsequent Church documents.

This distinction between "ministry" and "service" was slow to catch on in universities and ministry-formation programs. Many preferred the broader use. In the new millennium, however, the broader use gradually gave way to the more restricted use of the word "ministry."

This conversation about ministry and others like it gives an indication why catechesis took a back seat as the Church sifted out new ministerial issues.

Refocusing Parishes

The second aspect of looking beyond catechesis happened with the refocusing of parish organizations and ministries.

Parishes gave priority to pastoral councils, finance councils, social action committees, educational commissions, and worship committees, as pastors and ecclesial lay leaders refocused ministry in parishes. This affected the priority given to catechesis. Where religious education and schools formerly took top billing, now they competed for resources with other parish organizations.

Eventually, catechetical tensions settled down, and lines of responsibility were more clearly drawn. It was almost as if the particles and energies that exploded after Vatican II began to settle down. When the mushroom cloud dissipated, a shifting Catholic climate emerged. The commitment to solid catechetical content had not yet filtered into the catechetical enterprise. Adults educated in the late 1960s and 1970s knew little about basic Catholic beliefs, and some never regularly attended church beyond the eighth grade. When their children arrived, some parents failed to provide them with good examples of active commitment to the faith. While this was going on, catechetical leaders placed emphasis on adult faith formation. This did little to stem the tide of children and youths who were poorly educated in the faith.

Near the end of this decade, parishes clarified their approach to catechetical ministry. Dioceses developed clearer catechetical norms for elementary and secondary school religion teachers and catechists. At the same time, Catholic colleges and universities gave more attention to the Catholic identity of their schools. This reached its climax in the 1990s.

However, a persistent catechetical problem in parishes and schools remained. It centered on how to get students to attend catechetical sessions, and how to maintain their interest. This challenge continued as commitment to adult faith formation grew stronger, largely because of the Rite of Christian Initiation of Adults (RCIA). It presumed that a faith community existed and that people entering the RCIA were at various stages of faith. It provided a good way to catechize adults, but the search for ways to catechize children and youths continued with limited success.

By then, new catechetical leaders had emerged. They recognized the need for a systematic approach, but were intent on maintaining an experiential aspect. This meant that catechists had to apply the lessons to be learned to the faith levels of children and teenagers by taking into account their experiences. In some places, catechists did develop ways to keep students entertained, but taught them little.

Although diocesan requirements for catechists became more definite, many parishes lacked religion teachers or catechists who were well prepared. Instead, they used catechists who knew little themselves. When this happened, the catechized suffered and often dropped out of class, or learned little.

The solidification of catechetical content and approach wasn't easy to see right away in catechesis. It did not begin to take clear focus until after the publication of the *Catechism of the Catholic Church* in 1994 and the *General Directory for Catechesis* in 1997. Eventually, these two publications marked the end of an experimental time in catechesis, and the beginning of a new way to catechize.

Section 2:
MY CATECHETICAL JOURNEY

My connection with catechesis in the 1980s included university teaching, writing books, consulting with national organizations, research, lecturing on catechetics, and ministry in the United States and Canada. It also involved ministering in parishes. All of this kept me in close contact with parish and diocesan catechesis

A Change of Focus

When I left the Office of Religious Education in 1979, Archbishop Bernardin gave me a one-year sabbatical to attend the Religious Leader's Program at the University of Notre Dame. My goal on this sabbatical was to write a book about ministry and religious education in Catholic high schools. This book aimed to clarify hitherto ambiguous aspects of catechesis in Catholic high schools and in parishes. To this effect, I also wrote two small research books on religious education and catechesis, commissioned by the National Conference of Diocesan Directors of Religious Education (NCDD).

The NCDD disseminated these two books widely for use in dioceses and parishes. The first clarified the expressions "religious education" and "catechesis." Up to that time, Church documents used the term "catechesis," and academicians and religious educators often used "religious education" to describe the catechetical endeavor. The second book clarified the relationship between evangelization and catechesis.

These two works summarized the state of catechesis. The first book, *Religious Education and Catechesis: A Shift in Focus* (1981), described the tone of religious education in the early 1980s. The Introduction said:

> When I attended my first National Conference of Diocesan Directors of Religious Education Meeting in 1974, one director expressed concern about the wide

scope of the religious educator's responsibilities. He suggested that we might be better off if we concentrated on the catechetical dimension of our ministry.

His recommendation came at a time when religious educators on a diocesan and parish level were becoming involved in a variety of pastoral activities. These included: liturgical preparation, counseling, youth retreats, vocation work, social justice movements, and ministry to divorced and alienated Catholics. The parish religious educator often had responsibility for many pastoral activities while some diocesan offices resembled "mini chanceries."

The expression "total religious education" summed up the climate of the time and attitude of religious educators. It implied that religious education must: 1) take into account the whole person — body, soul, and spirit; 2) begin at birth and last until death; 3) relate to those societal patterns that influence a person's life — culture, family, ecumenical activities, parish or school programs, and many more. It also implied that: 1) wherever possible, diocesan religious education offices are in charge of religious education in the diocese, including the schools; 2) parish religious education employs a unified approach so that, if a Catholic school exists, there is no dichotomy between religious instruction in the school and out-of-school programs. (p. 1)

Interestingly enough, no mention was made here of the specific role of teaching the content of the faith, or of using adequate methods of faith formation. This hints at the climate of the times.

In this book, I suggested using the term "catechesis" instead of "religious education" to describe this ministry. Catechesis was the language of Church documents. The Church used the term "catechesis" instead of "religious education."

Initially, the suggestion to change the terminology of the official work of the NCDD from "religious education" to "catechesis" was met with considerable opposition from professional religious educators. After the NCDD accepted the book, gave its stamp of approval, and sold the book widely, the mentality of parish and diocesan religious educators shifted. It did not take long for them to begin using "catechesis," the language preferred by the Church.

In my book *Religious Education and Catechesis: A Shift in Focus,* I had noted that the expression "religious education" had been used only a few times in *Sharing the Light of Faith: National Catechetical Directory* (1979):

> The non-use of religious education terminology is a significant shift. It implies more than arguing about terminology since language is based upon fundamental attitudes and ways of acting. The basic orientation which the shift implies is toward more pastoral language, seen in a community context that brings catechesis into a direct relationship with the central ministries of the Church, especially evangelization, liturgy, and service. (p. 2)

Then it goes on to consider differences between catechesis and religious education.

The shift to catechesis is further described in my second book, *The Relationship between Evangelization and Catechesis,* written for the NCDD and published in 1981. This book used the terminology of catechesis and focused on the relationship between catechesis and evangelization. Church documents further nuanced these notions during the next fifteen years.

The Relationship between Evangelization and Catechesis was written after Pope Paul VI's apostolic exhortation, *Evangelii Nuntiandi* (*Evangelization in the Modern World*). I borrowed key ideas from this document and also from *Catechesi Tradendae* (*On Catechesis in Our Time*), the 1979 apostolic exhortation of Pope John Paul II.

The Relationship between Evangelization and Catechesis takes a holistic approach to evangelization, seeing it as the heart and soul of all ministries, and recognizing that other ministries are aspects of the evangelization process. It states that the risen Lord evangelizes through the Church community. For the Church, evangelization means:

> First of all to bear witness, in a simple and direct way, to God revealed in Jesus Christ, in the Holy Spirit, to bear witness that in his Son God has loved the world — that in his Incarnate Word he has given being to all things and has called men to eternal life. (*Evangelii Nuntiandi, 26*)

Seen in this way, "Evangelization is an ongoing process within the Christian community which seeks to initiate people ever more deeply into the mystery of God's love as manifested fully in the dying and rising of Jesus" (*The Relationship between Evangelization and Catechesis*, p. 6). This describes evangelization in a broad sense as an ongoing activity of the Christian community. Previously, it was held by many that evangelization is operative before a person makes a commitment to the faith. According to this broader view, all ministries are aspects of evangelization, including catechesis. Hence, effective catechesis evangelizes; so do liturgy and service ministries.

This is further illustrated in *Catechesi Tradendae,* when Pope John Paul II says:

> Evangelization — which has the aim of bringing the Good News to the whole of humanity, so that all may live by it — is a rich and complex, and dynamic reality, made up of elements, or one could say moments, that are essential and different from each other, and that must all be kept in view simultaneously. Catechesis is one of these moments — a very remarkable one — in the whole process of evangelization. (18)

When treating evangelization this way, catechists need to remember that "catechesis cannot exist without evangelization for its content is the same as the content of evangelization, namely the person and Gospel of Jesus Christ" (*Catechesi Tradendae,* 30).

During the 1980s, the religious educator slowly began to accept the language of catechesis and evangelization, although it was not until the 1990s that the Catholic community began to appreciate the real import of *Evangelii Nuntiandi.*

Teaching and Young Adults

Archbishop Bernardin assigned me to the Religious Studies Department at the University of Dayton in the fall of 1981.

I received the rank of associate professor. During the ensuing years, the challenges in academia became clear as professors worked to develop new approaches to ministry and catechesis. As this happened, students settled down and immersed themselves in their books. It was a new era, however, and their attitudes and orientation had shifted. Influenced by relativism and secular trends, it was difficult to convince students that absolute truths existed, and that some beliefs remain unchangeable, firm, and fixed.

Students often disagreed with professors who held to absolute norms of right and wrong. These young people would take the opposite stance, stressing individual conscience and denying that any absolutes existed. The rather superficial slogan, "follow your conscience," was the gauge of morality that many followed. Often, however, they had no clear idea of how to form a correct conscience. Some contended that it came down to a question of feelings.

In sharp contrast to the 1960s and early 1970s, when revolution, protest, long hair, and torn jeans were in the air, the students of the 1980s looked for careers that brought them success and earthly rewards. Many desired the good life, and some demanded more money as a starting salary than their professors made.

On the other hand, there were students who volunteered a year or more of their lives after graduation just to work in social ministries around the world. In the classroom or in private conversations, students opened their eyes and hearts when they believed that God called them to minister to the poor and downtrodden. Sometimes, they saw that this ministry could be offered as a nurse, doctor, teacher, social worker, or store operator.

Sadly, many students knew little about their Catholic faith. Some became upset when they learned how little they were taught about their religion as children and youths. Their lack of knowledge is testimony to the poor quality of parish catechesis or religious education in some Catholic schools and parishes. In my classes, I presumed little or no theological background from introductory level students. In contrast, students in graduate religious studies classes generally had a better background. They were hungry to find out what the Catholic Church taught, even though some had a weak commitment to remaining Catholics.

Through the 1980s, it was progressively more difficult to deal with Catholic graduate women students who had assimilated the liberalizing tendencies of feminism. Their inability to function in ordained Church ministries caused some to leave the Catholic community.

This was especially evident during summer sessions when students came from across the country. My courses centered on new ways to minster and catechize in parishes and schools. At the University of Dayton, we conducted a graduate institute on the *Catechism of the Catholic Church*, and invited scholars from different disciplines to address its implementation. Initially, the *Catechism* received mixed reviews in academia, as it did among many catechetical leaders.

The fuzzy and sometimes questionable theology taught even at universities led in 1990 to the publication of an ecclesial document from Pope John Paul II, *Ex Corde Ecclesiae* (*From the Heart of the Church*). This document gives directives on Catholic teaching and on the selection of professors in Catholic colleges and universities. The ambiguity at Catholic universities continued to filter down through graduate and undergraduate students into parishes and Catholic schools.

Traveling the Country

While teaching at the University of Dayton, I gave lectures around the country about once a month. These lectures included keynote addresses at conventions and workshops throughout the United States and Canada. Their content reflected the spirit of the times. Few sessions focused specifically on catechetical themes.

This became clear when I reviewed my lectures, which are now in the archives of the Archdiocese of Cincinnati. It was surprising to me that many lectures at national, regional, and diocesan religious education conventions did not pertain directly to catechesis. Rather, they focused on ministry in general. Instances of such lectures include:

At the Los Angeles Religious Education Congress (February 11-14, 1980), the topic was, "Healing, the Heart of Christian Ministry." Notable speakers at that conference included Rev. Regis Duffy, Rev. Carroll Stuhlmueller, and Gloria Durka. They addressed various dimensions of ministry and catechesis, with the emphasis on ministry. The same ministerial theme was reiterated in Tampa, Florida, and in Gaylord, Michigan, of the same year, when I was asked to speak on the topic of "What is Ministry." In Biloxi, Mississippi, and in Lake Charles, Louisiana, similar topics were featured.

Response to these conferences included a great deal of excitement and enthusiasm. Lay Catholics, religious men and women, and priests alike were searching for new ideas and solid materials to take back home. This was reflected in a February

18, 1980, letter from Bishop Bernard Law, Bishop of Spring-
field–Cape Girardeau. After a three-day session for that diocese, he wrote me saying:

> Just a word to let you know how thoroughly I appre-
> ciated your presentations at the Religious Education
> Institute, and how delighted I was to get to spend
> some extended time with you.

The 1980s were exciting years, as the Church headed in
new directions in an effort to produce something worthwhile
for ministry and catechesis. Needless to say, the question of
Catholic orthodoxy caused bishops to be more selective in inviting speakers into their dioceses.

The theme of ministry continued through the 1980s.
My presentations fit into the overall focus on ministry. In
1982, at the Denver Mile-High Religious Education Congress, my keynote address was "Ministry: A Call to Give
and Receive." Six months later, my course at the University
of San Francisco was titled "Theology of Pastoral Ministry."
On June 27, 1984, an address at the Ursuline Symposium
in Pepper Pike, Ohio, was called "Ministry, Leadership, and
Catholic Schools." "Ministry" was the topic of the decade.
These lecture titles indicate just how strong this theme was
during the 1980s.

By the middle of the decade, the notion of ministry became more nuanced. A review of archival materials indicates
that the lectures were moving inward, to a deeper spiritual
realm. This was symptomatic of a call of the Spirit that ministers, including catechists, were feeling. A brief sample of my
talk titles reflects this inward movement. Note the following

titles: "Ministry, Reconciliation, and Leadership" (San Bernardino, California, 1985); "Catholic School Ministry and the Kingdom of God" (Iowa Catholic Schools Week, 1985); "Walking in the Footsteps of Jesus" (Cincinnati Religious Education Congress, 1987); and "Tomorrow's Parish: New Wine in New Wineskins" (Salt Lake City Congress, 1987).

This inward movement and the lack of specific catechetical content during this time is also suggested in two letters sent to me after a lecture tour. They are quoted here without names and places. The first one reads:

> It has been great. The input was rich. The process was a good blend of input from you and drawing on the experiences of the group. Most of all, it was you yourself, your person that was the great gift and sharing.

Notice the focus of the writer is on experience, sharing, and an inner orientation. During this time, attendees at these conferences were interested in learning how what they heard would help them to be better persons, parents, ministers, and catechists. The second letter reads:

> The feeling of hope and sharing of the need for healing and forgiveness at the assembly is very much deeply impressed in my heart by Fr. Bob Hater, which I'll impress to my students.

Here again, this person clearly wanted to share the notion of reconciliation in the classroom. This took precedence over my remarks on the importance of teaching the basic beliefs of the Church. Religious education congress developers and diocesan leaders recognized this need and invited speakers to address similar topics. As a result, the attendees could bring the process of healing into their families, parishes, and classrooms. This points out where the Church was during this time.

As the 1980s drew to a close, fresh ministerial themes started to appear. Most notably, these included parish revitalization, lay ministries, evangelization, family, and some specific aspects of catechesis. My addresses at catechetical conferences included ""Lay Ministry" (Sidney Ohio Religious Education Congress Keynote, 1986), "Evangelization: Call to the Kingdom" (Los Angeles Religious Education Congress, February 5-6, 1988), "Parish Revitalization" (Baton Rouge, Louisiana, Religious Education Congress Keynote, 1987), "Effective Parish Religious Education for Children and Youth" (National Catholic Education Association Congress, Denver, Colorado, February 11, 1988), and "Family" (Steubenville, Ohio, 1988).

I was able to evaluate the state of catechetical ministry firsthand, as I conducted workshops for pastoral ministers, addressed priests' assemblies, and taught in Catholic colleges and universities across this country and in Canada. Everywhere, the story was similar: priests and religious educators were struggling to find effective ways to catechize adults, youth, and children in the beliefs of the Church as the emerging new ministries occupied them.

Section 3:
TRENDS AND CONCLUSIONS FROM THIS PERIOD

Certain conclusions can be drawn from this period that help us to understand and enhance catechesis. These are as follows.

1. Strengthen the content of catechesis.

In the 1980s, as a clearer picture emerged, catechists, parents, priests, and the Church hierarchy recognized the need to strengthen the content of religious instruction. This was done on a diocesan level, in part, by the development of graded courses of studies that were used to measure the acceptability of various textbooks. This occurred at the same time that new methods for catechizing were developed. (See Hater, *New Visions, New Directions*, fn. 16) These methods linked teaching Catholic beliefs and practices to a person's everyday life. Such developments were incorporated into the catechetical life of the Catholic community.

2. Clarify the role of evangelization and catechesis.

Clarifying the proper role of catechetical ministry was assisted by new developments in Catholic evangelization, especially those presented in *Evangelii Nuntiandi* (1975). Catechists clearly saw the important role that evangelization plays in the Church's catechetical ministry. Influenced also by *Catechesi Tradendae* (1979), they viewed catechesis as an element or moment in the evangelization process. This process is rooted in the Christian community where the Lord continues to proclaim the message of God's love. Catechesis cannot exist without evangelization since its content is the same as the content of evangelization — namely, the person and Gospel of Jesus Christ.

Evangelization is the energizing center of all pastoral ministries, including catechesis. Pope Paul VI described it as the "essential mission of the Church" (*EN*, 4) which provides the motivating force for all Church ministries. Catechesis has a special relationship to evangelization, as is described in *Catechesi Tradendae*, which was quoted earlier:

> Evangelization — which has the aim of bringing the
> Good News to the whole of humanity, so that all may
> live by it — is a rich, complex, and dynamic reality,
> made up of elements, or one could say moments, that
> are essential and different from each other, and that
> must all be kept in view simultaneously. Catechesis is
> one of these moments — a very remarkable one — in
> the whole process of evangelization. (18)

To better appreciate the relationship of evangelization and catechesis, we summarize the relationship of informal and systematic catechesis, and consider their relationship to the catechetical process.

"Informal catechesis" includes pastoral activities — family prayer, speaking of God's love, community building, evangelizing activities, service projects, and liturgy. Even if not intended primarily to catechize, these all have a catechetical aspect. To qualify as catechesis, these activities have to relate in some way to God and to the Christian story.

On the other hand, "systematic catechesis" is definite and orderly. It involves any catechetical activities that aim at calling forth a response to the living Word of God in a deliberate, intentional, and structured way.

The expression "catechetical process" is often used to describe the method that catechesis employs. Regardless of its form, it takes into account the situation of the person catechized and applies basic teaching to a person's life situation. In so doing, the catechist encourages the catechized to consider the basic teachings and see how new insights can be integrated into life. One aim of this process is to elicit a positive response in the person's life and worship.

3. Recognize the special relationship between evangelization and catechesis.

Focusing on the relationship between evangelization and catechesis made it easier for catechists to see that conversion is lifelong, and that Jesus' message must be related to a person's life experiences. This led catechists to stress Scripture and to incorporate the Gospel's justice dimension into all catechetical activities. It also helped them to recognize the importance of taking into account the psychological and spiritual state of the catechized.

As catechists learned better ways to balance content and method, it became obvious that conversion and methods to help facilitate it were not the same thing. The goal of catechesis is conversion, but there are many different methods to enhance it. Within the context of conversion, it also became clear that knowledge about one's faith (content or message) is an important part of conversion.

A variety of adult faith formation efforts entered the scene. The Catholic laity increasingly prepared themselves to take a responsible role in the Church and in secular society. This preparation often happened through small group sharing sessions. These included Christ Renews His Parish, RENEW, Marriage Encounter, Charismatic movements, and Scripture study groups, as well as other parish and diocesan programs.

As Catholic renewal proceeded, Church members experienced the trauma of change, the demands of freedom, and the responsibilities of conscience. But they also learned how to relate to the secular world and to other religious denominations. The Church stood at a turning point and took another look at how the Christian community influences the lifelong process of coming to faith. As this happened, Catholics discovered anew the implications of evangelization for catechetical ministry.

4. Recast the Catholic story.

Pre-Vatican II Catholicism cast the Catholic story within the parameters of the institutional Church. This clearly spelled out a Catholic's identity as a member of the one, true Church. Catholics went to Mass each Sunday, confessed their sins to a priest frequently, abstained from meat on Fridays, and knew the teachings of the *Baltimore Catechism*. The Church, through educational endeavors, taught the content of the Catholic faith. Often, studying and reading Scripture privately was discouraged. We were told what it meant to be human, Christian, and Catholic. We knew our story and accepted it.

At Vatican II, the Catholic story was recast to present the Church as a community — the People of God. In the evolution of our story's adaptation, the teaching of the basics of the faith sometimes became blurred. Many gray or confusing areas surfaced since some interpretations of the emerging Catholic story were not consistent or precise.

The new theology, coming after the council, shifted the roles of the laity, hierarchy, priests, and religious. It also changed the interpretations of some of the Church's message. The Catholic community gained new insights about God's presence in nature, people, and other religions. At the same time, Catholic biblical, doctrinal, moral, and pastoral theology also changed. Renewed appreciation of Scripture encouraged Catholics to apply the biblical message to life. They learned that Jesus proclaimed the kingdom of God and that He invites people to live the message of God's kingdom in their families, work, parishes, and dioceses. In the more open Church that emerged, pre-Vatican II practices changed, and theological and pastoral perspectives were refocused. But, the basic beliefs of Catholicism remained unchanged.

The core of the Catholic story and the call to become a catechist "begins with Christ," as Pope Francis says (*Address to the International Catechetical Congress*, September 27, 2013). From Jesus' life and teachings, all Christian traditions have emerged. As the *Catechism of the Catholic Church* says:

> At the heart of catechesis is a person, Jesus of Nazareth, the Father's only Son, who suffered and died for us and, after rising from the dead, now lives with us forever. (426)

The Catholic story is ritualized in worship. It emerges from the collective, fundamental attitudes of Catholics, from the mythos, the patterns of basic beliefs, developed over the centuries. These attitudes are lived out and celebrated in ritual activities, such as baptism, Eucharist, and various expressions of the Catholic lifestyle.

Communal or personal faith develops from the interplay of the Catholic story and its ritualization. In this way, the community and individuals say "Yes" to this story. Simply put, faith is a person's or a group's "Amen" to the Catholic story. This ownership of the story, in turn, moves a person or community to live according to the dictates of the story.

The creeds, codes, and other formulations of belief developed from the Catholic story and its ritualization. Striving to understand the faith and the fundamental core of community belief (content statements) through rational study is a valuable way to clarify the Catholic story. But, by itself, it never establishes identity.

Identity is forged in the interplay of the story and its ritualization in the faith history and experience of a community of believers. The content of the story can express only what happens on a deeper level. It is always an inadequate approximation of the mystery that roots the relationship of God and the Catholic community.

Since the Catholic faith begins in Jesus' story, one cannot read, interpret, or understand the *Catechism of the Catholic Church* apart from His story. Christ must be at the center of all catechesis. Neither can a catechist or anyone else effectively catechize, if he or she does not know the story of Jesus. Consequently, catechesis begins with Jesus' story as it is revealed in Scripture and is handed down in the authentic living witness of the Catholic tradition.

5. Develop flexible adult faith formation.

Adult faith formation takes into account the experience and circumstances of adult learners. This is central in developing any viable approach for catechizing adults. To help in this important catechetical outreach, *Adult Catechesis in the Christian Community* was published in 1990 by the International Council for Catechesis. This effort encouraged catechists to show particular concern for people living in irregular situations.

Irregular situations can occur in many circumstances — in marriages and through immigration, to name two. Catechists are to reach out to such people. Many times, when people return to the Church for more faith formation — such as when parents return when their children receives first Communion — other issues are involved. In such cases:

> Above all, one must begin by accepting adults where they are.... It is essential to keep in mind the specific adults with whom one is working, their cultural background, human and religious needs, their expectations, faith experiences, and their potential. It is also important to be attentive to their marital and professional status. (*Adult Catechesis in the Christian Community: Some Principles and Guidelines,* International Council for Catechesis, 55-57, Vatican City, 1990)

The *Catechism of the Catholic Church* makes no decisions about effective teaching methodologies. This is left up to the skills, background, wisdom, and experience of the catechist. To help devise effective methodologies, the document *Informative Dossier on the Catechism of the Catholic Church* was prepared and distributed by the Vatican-appointed editorial commission which oversaw the writing of the *Catechism.*

This dossier encourages catechists to take seriously the cultural situations of the catechized. Parents, catechists, and others are to devise effective ways to teach basic Catholic beliefs according to the ages, circumstances, and cultures of the catechized (*Dossier,* p. 22). In other words, the *Catechism of the Catholic Church* is to use the positive developments in catechesis that emerged after Vatican II.

In reiterating the importance of adapting doctrinal content, the *Catechism* says:

Such indispensable adaptation, required by the differences of culture, age, spiritual life, and social and ecclesial condition among the People of God, belongs to other catechisms following on this work, and is the particular task of those who teach the faith. (24)

The dossier indicated that there are limits to the *Catechism,* which, it says, is "one of the means of catechesis, which, in its turn, is one of the ways of carrying out the prophetic ministry, which in union with the priestly and kingly ministries, constitutes the mission of the Church" (*Dossier,* 28). Although the *Catechism* is a thorough, scholarly, and pastoral means of catechesis, it is not the only means.

6. Catechesis is more than learning facts and memorizing.

Teaching the basic truths of the faith is an important aspect of the Catholic story. For this reason, the early Christian Church formulated beliefs and creeds. The *Acts of the Apostles* recounts Peter's testimony on Pentecost and spells out core Christian beliefs:

Jesus the Nazarene was a man commended by God by the miracles and portents and signs that God worked through him when he was among you, as you all know. This man, who was put into your power by the deliberate intention and foreknowledge of God, you took and had crucified by men outside of the Law. You killed him, but God raised him to life…. Now raised to the heights by God's right hand, he has received from the Father the Holy Spirit, who was promised, and what you see and hear is the outpouring of that Spirit." (2:22-23, Jerusalem Bible)

The Christian Scriptures recounted foundational Christian beliefs while Church councils, liturgical formulas, creeds, popes, bishops, and theologians clarified these beliefs.

Cultures and languages affect the attitudes and images that people use to express foundational beliefs. Hence, the intellectualization of beliefs in creed, code, or theological formulas is not the whole picture. Rational expressions of belief, in themselves, cannot establish Catholic identity. Identity happens in the interplay of the Christian story, its ritualization, and the faith response of Christians.

The Church needed to clarify essential Catholic beliefs and establish benchmarks, reflecting key elements of the Catholic belief system. Teaching the creeds, codes, or other formulations of belief without rooting such teachings in a person's life and in Church life and rituals makes little sense where conversion is concerned. It may have value when studying about religious beliefs, but little value when the intention is to elicit or deepen faith.

Church teachings are connected to the heart of the Catholic community's beliefs and practices. They solidify and clarify what a person may only have vaguely perceived. For example, a young person may have experienced family love and parish faith rituals, centering on Jesus. But, the meaning of such experiences may be vague in his or her life until the individual learns about Jesus, the Church, and why Catholics believe as they do.

This element of clarification was often missing in post-Vatican II catechesis. Consequently, many youths and adults learned in a vague way what it meant to be Catholic but had little knowledge to substantiate *why* or *what* they believed. Centering Catholic teachings in Jesus' story gives Catholics a clearer understanding of what is essential to their belief and what is peripheral.

The Church has traditionally taught Catholic Christian beliefs by relating how the belief connects to the story of Jesus. For example, belief in devotion to the saints is important, but is not nearly as central to the message of the Gospels as is Jesus' teaching on social justice.

7. Catholic story — beyond the facts.

After Vatican II, teaching the basics of the faith was sometimes minimized. While the Catholic story goes beyond facts, learning the facts does play a vital role in developing Catholic identity. Catholics learn who they are through living witnesses of faith, and by learning what Jesus and the Church teach. This requires the ability to understand and to express basic elements of the faith.

Catechists have asked, "What about memorization?" People memorize facts in history, science, and mathematics. Why not in religion? It's true that Catholics need to know prayers, Scripture, creeds, and basic teachings. Short formulae of faith are valuable ways to clarify basic Catholic teaching. In saying this, however, it is important to remember that memorization, alone, does not produce faith that is "living, conscious, and active" (*Documents of Vatican II*, "Bishops Office in the Church," 14).

Catechists in the 1980s knew that returning to the catechism's memorization method was not the answer. This method had its limitations. Among other things, it favored those who were good at memorization and put those who were not at a disadvantage. In addition, it did not foster faith formation in children, youths, or adults. The catechism approach also did not emphasize Scripture. Additionally, short answers to key questions leave important issues unlearned.

Religious educators saw that effective catechetical methods incorporated other aspects of catechesis. Benchmarks of Catholic knowledge gained through memorization did provide Catholics with a stable core of knowledge analogous to that afforded Protestants who memorized biblical passages. In fact, memorizing Scripture passages shouldn't be reserved just for Protestants. Catholics can memorize key passages from Scripture and basic Church teachings to help ground their Catholic faith.

While many catechists advocated some memorization, another question remained: "Why should we have people memorize?" The answer is simple and timeless. Memorization of facts is necessary because memory helps root a person's identity and put together the big picture. For Catholics, this big picture centers on Jesus, the Trinity, the Church, and knowledge of the faith tradition. These are essential for understanding the wisdom and meaning of Catholicism, and for critical reflection upon the Catholic faith or particular aspects of belief and practice.

A person's ability to reflect on his or her faith is important. In an open society, Catholic adults must frequently assess situations and make moral decisions in the light of their beliefs and traditions. Memorization is a tool to provide knowledge to help Catholics face the many challenges of today's world. It can also help in a person's devotional life. Coupled with Scripture, it provides a rich source of meditation and helps us to relate God's Word to everyday experiences.

The gradual solidification that emerged in this Third Period set the foundation for what came in the Fourth Period. A greater appreciation of what went before put catechists in a better position. They were able to move more positively into the future and avoid the mistakes of the past.

CHAPTER 5

SYSTEMATIC – EXPERIENTIAL PERIOD

(1990s to the Present)

> "Helping children, young people, and adults to get to know and love God more and more and more is one of the most beautiful educational adventures you can have."
>
> (Pope Francis, *Address to International Catechetical Congress*, September 27, 2013)

The worst of the explosion resulting from Vatican II-inspired changes dissipated in the 1990s. Bishops, priests, and sisters leading the post-Vatican II changes in the Church were getting older or retiring. A more traditional, younger generation of Catholic, clergy, religious, bishops, and laity emerged.

In the years after Vatican II, Catholics still had to sift out what being a Catholic meant as the Church adopted a more traditional stance. The persistent question among them remained, "What makes a Catholic different?" To answer this question, catechetical leaders, bishops, and their representatives focused on more systematic approaches to catechesis. They stressed basic beliefs but remained open to connecting these beliefs to the experiences of the catechized. Hence, we use the expression "Systematic – Experiential Period" to describe this era.

This chapter is divided into three sections. Section 1 considers historical background. Section 2 treats my personal journey, and Section 3 summarizes the conclusions and insights about this period that were presented in this chapter.

Section 1:
HISTORICAL PERSPECTIVES

Increasingly, secular values challenged renewal in Catholic beliefs and teachings. More Catholics left the Church, and Catholicism saw the growth of a minority of clergy and laity whose Catholic views and devotional lives were much more traditional. Among them, young Catholics — both lay and clerical — wanted to know what they had missed, before all the changes inspired by Vatican II took place.

Although increasing in ecclesial influence, these traditional Catholics were small in numbers. Many, claiming to be more faithful than the average Catholic, took Pope John Paul II as their model. This group had a certain view of what it meant to be a good Catholic. They believed it meant frequent Mass attendance, frequent reception of the Sacrament of Penance and Reconciliation, Marian devotions, Perpetual Adoration, theological orthodoxy, and following the teaching of Popes John Paul II and Benedict XVI.

To appreciate the shifting Church climate, we consider the larger cultural context which affected the Catholic attitude. Creeping secularization engulfed our country and continued to intensify. This had a profound effect on Catholic cultural and religious values. It also brought with it a growing anti-religious sentiment and the growth of atheism.

Secularization in the United States and Europe, and in Third World countries, increased dramatically after 1990 as a result of the technological explosion. As activities for adults and teenagers increased, it was difficult to get them to attend catechetical sessions. Many parishes hired youth ministers, hoping to connect with teenagers in different ways that reached beyond catechetical sessions alone.

In addition to secularization, immigration also had a profound impact during this period. Because Americans were known as a free people, this country attracted immigrants from many different ethnic backgrounds. The race, ethnicity, class, and religion of these newcomers affected our culture. In addition to the immigrant influx, the culture was also affected by increased terror from crime, struggles with health care, growing poverty, and technological growth.

After the Iron Curtain came down, countries once under tight Communist rule became free. At about the same time, the influence of Islam grew and was felt around the world. These developments affected Christianity worldwide. While the number of Catholics grew dramatically in countries south of the equator, the traditional Catholic population, excluding immigrants, decreased in Europe and the United States. The influx of people into the United States from Third World countries increased. In particular, these people were often undocumented immigrants from countries south of our border. As our cultural composition became more varied and complex, the resulting picture was a rich and colorful mosaic of different peoples, cultures, and faiths.

Naturally, catechists had to face new challenges in integrating the ethnic backgrounds of new immigrants into their catechetical lessons. Catechists were now ministering to newly arrived Catholic ethnic groups who were often more traditional in their Catholic faith. This was difficult for volunteer catechists with little formal training. Nonetheless, the new immigrants fit in well with the growing conservative trend seen in the broader Church.

From the year 2000 forward, catechetical conferences continued to offer a majority of lectures and workshops on various ministerial themes. They did not focus narrowly on the content of what Catholics believe. For instance, in 2004, my keynote address at the Newark Forum was "Partners in Evangelization: Family, Work, and Church." In 2007, at the Raleigh, North Carolina, Conference, my theme was "Finding God in the Stories of Our Lives." I used the same topic to address the University of Dallas Ministry Conference in 2008. Gradually, however, as the first decade of the new millennium came to a close, there was a shift. I began to see more concentration on basic Catholic beliefs at major conferences, such as at the Fashion Me a People Conference in Orlando, Florida, in 2009.

Before the 1990s, the catechetical books and approaches used in parishes and Catholic schools varied widely. This was clear as I dealt with national speakers, textbook publishers, attendees at major religious education conventions, catechetical leaders, and college professors. This changed, however, and the change was led by the bishops. Their Subcommittee on the Catechism began to make more precise requirements for religion textbooks to be found in conformity with the *Catechism of the Catholic Church.*

Cultural Context

Effective catechesis demanded that the Church's basic teachings address the changing Catholic population. Catechists had to keep in mind our country's growing diversity and the issues of freedom, mobility, materialism, individuality, technological growth, and moral insensitivity. We should take a look at these issues to see how they impacted the catechetical climate.

Diversity

Diversity intensified at the end of the second millennium. It led to conflicting positions, relativism, and moral insensitivity. Society faced quandaries resulting from such positions, which sometimes meant trying to reconcile opposing values. Too often, there was a shortage of consistent "moral glue" that was needed to uphold society's moral fabric.

Such diversity affected catechesis. Catholic book publishers wondered how to address their books to different ethnic groups. When books were to be published in Spanish, they worried about what pictures should be used. At least seven different Hispanic populations were target audiences for the books. Catechists increasingly faced challenges to relate their catechetical lessons to the various cultures of the catechized.

Freedom

The culture of the United States rests on the basic foundation of human freedom as it was established by the Constitution. Few other countries give citizens and noncitizens alike the rights that we have. These rights, sometimes drawn out endlessly in court systems, are based on a person's inalienable right to life, liberty, and the pursuit of happiness.

Freedom guarantees the rights of individuals and churches to practice their religion of choice. In the aftermath of Vatican II, cultural attitudes toward freedom in the United States affected Catholics. As the Church moved to a more open society, many Catholics formed their own consciences on matters of morals, discipline, and belief. Some took seriously the teachings of the Church, while others did not.

Catholics scrutinized theological, political, and social issues in light of their personal choices. This put stress on Church leaders. They were now faced with Catholics who no longer agreed with their directives.

While celebrating the blessings of freedom, it helps to recall the words of the *Catechism of the Catholic Church*:

> As long as freedom has not bound itself definitely to its ultimate good which is God, there is the possibility of choosing between good and evil, and thus of growth in perfection or of failing and sinning.... There is no true freedom except in the service of what is good and just. (1732-1733)

Catholics increasingly recognized the challenges of exercising their freedom in responsible ways. This meant looking prophetically at how the Lord seemed to be leading them to salvation through the Catholic community and her teachings. For catechists, this meant teaching the catechized to respect the Church's authority. They also had to teach Catholics how to form one's conscience while making sure they knew what and why the Church teaches what it teaches. This could only happen when catechists knew basic Catholic teachings themselves.

Individuality

Individuality is not to be confused with individualism. Individualism is a self-centered concern with oneself to the exclusion of others. Individuality, on the other hand, is a recognition of our personal importance that never minimizes other people. Catechists are to help the catechized discover their uniqueness before God, and teach them how God gives different gifts to different people.

Mobility

From the earliest days of our nation's history, the citizens of the United States have been very mobile. Impelled by a frontier spirit, they migrated from coastal regions to plains, mountains, and deserts. This expansion continued into the new frontiers made possible by technology. Today, this same spirit enables people of various cultures to communicate personally and to "travel" electronically around the world in ways that were not possible a generation ago.

Mobility certainly brought new challenges to parishes, and its effects on catechesis were profound. Since long-term contact with a parish community does not happen with mobile people, it is important to encourage parishioners to find a firm anchor in their faith. This anchoring must go beyond one particular parish.

Materialism

As the new millennium approached, Catholics realized that neither certitude nor happiness is found in a materialistic way of life. They understood that the teachings of Jesus certainly challenged a worldly lifestyle. Materialism holds up the latest car, clothes, or iPads as necessary for a happy, successful life. Often, television implies that success is associated with pleasure, products, and possessions. It is important for catechists to counter this message through their catechesis. They must teach that Catholic certitude can come from Scripture, Catholic teaching, a new appreciation of parish community, and a healthy regard for Church leaders.

Technology

Technology has made great strides forward in revolutionizing the world. It enables people to keep more accurate records, build safer buildings, develop comfortable work spaces, and communicate instantly through fax machines, interactive video, telephones, and computers. Advances in medicine also help people to live longer, healthier lives. Technology enables us to travel worldwide in short time spans. We can communicate globally, and enjoy the benefits of a free society. Catechists need to take advantage of these great blessings of technology. Among other things, the Internet and social media have challenged Catholics to work for social justice so that all people can benefit from technology. Catechists are to use these technological innovations to help the catechized learn more about God, their dignity, and responsibilities to others.

Moral Sensitivity

Moral sensitivity is necessary for Christians to resist negative secular influences. Those who stand up for what they believe and live by the values they preach offer a powerful witness to society. Countering moral insensitivity demands faithfulness to Jesus' moral teachings. While respecting the rights of individuals to form their own consciences, catechists were challenged in the 1990s to clearly present the Church's teachings and help those catechized learn how to form a correct conscience.

Changing Parish Organization

During the time frame discussed in this chapter, Catholic identity was affected by the closing and consolidation of parishes which was largely brought on by the priest shortage. Up to this time, for most Catholics, Catholic life in this country often centered on just one parish. Bonding with a single parish rooted Catholic life in a particular place and community. Recalling a parish where one grew up or worshiped later in life reminded many Catholics of certain statues, the altar, confessional, pews, or a beloved pastor. Many Catholics also remembered their first Communions or weddings in these parishes.

The consolidation or closing of parishes changed this internal dynamic associated with Catholic identity. How does a person connect closely with a parish cluster, parish region, or a merged parish? Where no such identity exists, it's harder for catechists to help the catechized recognize the stable community that the Church can provide. The change of parish structures deeply influenced Catholics, often more than pastors or diocesan leaders realized. It fractured the Catholic climate that some held on to when they considered their Catholic identity.

Catechism of the Catholic Church

The U.S. bishops strongly supported the call of Pope John Paul II to develop a new catechism. The intent was to bring unity and stability to catechesis on a worldwide basis. Even though catechesis stabilized in the 1980s, unrest continued during the publication of the *Catechism of the Catholic Church* (1994) and the *General Directory for Catechesis* (1997).

Many professional catechists in the United States opposed the development of this catechism and its final form in English. It provided difficulty for many women DREs and other Church ministers because of its noninclusive language. Although this issue continues to provide challenges to professional religious educators, many read it as if inclusive language were used. One reader of this book remarked, "If one does not see oneself in what the *Catechism* says, how can it be relevant?"

Before the publication of the *Catechism of the Catholic Church* there was limited supervision over Catholic textbook companies and over diocesan and parish catechetical leaders. Most took their responsibilities seriously, but it became clear that more oversight of what was taught was necessary. Content, rather than methodology, needed to be strengthened.

This is illustrated in one conversation with a bishop who was the ordinary of his diocese. We spoke at length at a convocation for priests. As we discussed the role of priests and bishops in the teaching of religion, I shared my perspective. I said to the bishop, "I get the impression that the United States bishops are now taking more responsibility for catechesis than in the years immediately after Vatican II." He looked at me in a determined way and answered strongly: "You got it right, Bob. The bishops are taking back religious education and catechesis. We will change the climate in the Church that has led to twenty-five years of content-less religious education. The *Catechism of the Catholic Church* is the first step in this effort."

Whether one agrees with his assessment of "content-less religious education" or not, his words were prophetic of the years that followed. After the publication of the *Catechism*, the climate of catechesis changed significantly under the direction of Rome and the U.S. bishops. They insisted that catechetical teaching must be consistent with the content and language of the *Catechism*.

Subcommittee on the Catechism

Clarification of basic teachings used in every catechetical course took place after the initial establishment of the Ad Hoc Committee to Oversee the Use of the Catechism. The U.S. bishops formed this committee to ensure the accuracy and completeness of catechetical materials approved for use on elementary and secondary levels.

The chair of the original bishops' committee invited me to evaluate textbooks during my tenure as professor of religious studies at the University of Dayton. Because of other responsibilities, I declined the offer. After the committee was set up, a textbook series seeking conformity with the *Catechism of the Catholic Church* was sent by the bishops' committee to several specially selected theologians to be evaluated by them for approval. The books needed to follow the protocols established for conformity with the *Catechism*. Once a textbook was found to be in conformity, the publishers could put the following note on the top left page in the beginning of each book:

The Ad Hoc Committee to Oversee the Use of the
Catechism, United States Conference of Catholic
Bishops, has found this catechetical text, copyright
[year], to be in conformity with the *Catechism of the
Catholic Church.*

The inclusion of multiple protocols (required basic teachings to be included in the book under consideration), established by the U.S. bishops 'conference, influenced whether a
book was approved or not. Initially, the Ad Hoc Committee
required that all the necessary content of the *Catechism* be included. Later on, the requirements became more specific and
the committee required that the language used in the textbooks be in conformity with the language of the *Catechism.*
This meant that the language of catechesis was to follow a more
classic language, analogous to the uniform language that students once learned from the *Baltimore Catechism.* Today this
committee is called the "Subcommittee on the Catechism."

In addition to content and language conformity, the bishops required that the textbooks satisfy the criteria of authenticity and completeness. This means they need to have a Trinitarian focus, a Christological centrality, and an ecclesial context.
They must also treat the sacraments within the Paschal Mystery, and present the moral life in the personal and social teachings of the Church as a new life in the Spirit. The committee
also mandated that approved texts include the Church's teachings on the dignity of the human person within the context of
the Fifth Commandment. In addition, the textbooks had to be
biblically balanced, including passages from both the Old and
New Testaments, and soteriological in orientation. That meant

that these books needed to be directed to the Church's teaching on salvation.

Initially, these protocols received mixed reviews by religious educators. Those accustomed to their own ways of teaching often objected. This group included some high school religion teachers in Catholic schools, but also parish catechists. Younger teachers and those who had started teaching more recently were generally more receptive to the protocols and the use of the *Catechism*. For many, it became their main reference book. This happened, in part, because younger catechists and high school religion teachers belonged to a generation that was more traditional in its personal beliefs and practices.

The requirements of the Subcommittee on the Catechism challenged textbook publishers to develop more exact language and to devise fresh approaches to catechize students. It was challenging for catechists to present orthodox, Catholic teaching while maintaining student interest.

From the time the Ad Hoc Committee was established, textbook publishers were far more diligent in presenting Church teaching in an accurate and complete way. Some could not afford the added expenses and ceased publishing religion textbooks. If a publisher sought approval for conformity and did not receive it, it cost a lot of money in lost sales as well as added money to revise the books before applying again for conformity.

The bishops accomplished their goal of making sure that student books contained orthodox Catholic teaching. In the past, some parents complained that textbooks did not contain enough basic Church teachings. Later, the opposite objection was heard. Some critics claimed that the language of the books was not understandable or consistent with the language that young people use.

Regardless of any limitations it may have, the *Catechism* was a milestone in developing catechesis worldwide. Especially in the United States, its publication marked a shift in how catechesis was handled. Coupled with the *General Directory of Catechesis*, it set the tone of future catechesis. Together, these two books stressed the melding of solid, basic Catholic teachings and good methodology.

General Directory for Catechesis

The need for overall directives in catechesis was met with the publication of the *General Directory for Catechesis* (*GDC*) in 1997. It was a revision of the *General Catechetical Directory* (*GCD*), originally approved and promulgated by Pope Paul VI in 1971. The earlier directory was foundational and served to focus post-Vatican II catechesis. In the ensuing years, other Church documents added clarity to what it said. New insights were gleaned from effective catechists and succeeding ecclesial documents, especially *Evangelii Nuntiandi, Catechesi Tradendae*, and the *Catechism of the Catholic Church*. This prompted the revision of the GCD. The revision was undertaken by the Vatican's Congregation for the Clergy and was named the *General Directory for Catechesis*. It contextualized catechesis within the evangelization process, as *Evangelii Nuntiandi* advocated. It also focused the content of faith contained in the *Catechism of the Catholic Church*.

The *General Directory for Catechesis* brought a new orientation into the catechetical enterprise. This document was generally acclaimed as a solid tool for the revitalization of catechesis on all levels.

Clergy Scandal

It's a sad irony that in the same era the Church was working hard to clarify catechesis, the clergy sex abuse scandal rocked the Church to it foundations. This deeply wounded the overall spirit and vitality of the Catholic Church. Anger and frustration, along with a questioning of the authority of bishops and priests, ensued. This scandal led to a diminished trust in the clergy, especially in parishes and dioceses hard hit by the scandal. This substantial erosion of confidence continued into the next millennium. It greatly affected the laity's trust, and diminished the Church's authority in all aspects of ministry, including catechesis.

In light of the hurt, alienation, and disaffection of many Catholics from the Church, Pope Francis' words in August 2013 are hopefully prophetic. "I see clearly," the pope said, "that the thing the Church needs most today is the ability to heal the wounds and to warm the hearts of the faithful: it needs nearness, proximity." His comments, part of an interview with Fr. Antonio Spadaro, SJ, were published in *America* magazine's September 30, 2013, issue. Hopefully, his words are a rallying cry, needed to move the Church, as a whole, and individual Christians toward reconciliation and forgiveness.

Into the Third Millennium

The third millennium saw a developing trend among American citizens. The beginning of the twenty-first century witnessed a more traditional lifestyle approach in our society. The liberals of the 1970s and 1980s were retiring, replaced by more business-oriented, goal-directed citizens who had a desire for the good life. The bombing of the Twin Towers in New York on September 11, 2001, and successive wars in Iraq, Afghanistan, and other hot spots around the world shook our global culture. The spirit of the United States changed. This was followed by the recession of 2007, massive immigration into the United States from the Southern Hemisphere, unemployment, and the housing crisis.

After the year 2000, the movement toward a more conservative Catholicism grew stronger. Bishops appointed after Vatican II were gradually replaced by bishops whom some people called "John Paul II bishops," or "Benedict XVI bishops." Many younger priests and seminarians referred to themselves as John Paul II or Benedict XVI priests or seminarians. Many of these men chose to wear the cassock. They promoted traditional devotions and Perpetual Adoration. They looked with caution on much of the theology that came out of Vatican II. They said, "We intend to correct abuses and mistakes that happened after Vatican II, and make things right again." It didn't take them long after ordination to realize that things were much more complex than they imagined. They soon realized that the Catholic laity had come of age. Lay people were not going to blindly follow their directions.

A similar trajectory occurred in lay-ministry-formation programs and among younger Catholics. It was reflected in the Catholic home-school movement. It largely consisted of traditional Catholics, many wishing to return to what was lost at Vatican II. For some, this included the Latin Mass.

At national and diocesan religious education conventions, this move to traditionalism was apparent in the books published, the speakers invited, and those attending. These conferences were attended largely by lay ministers, and by only a few religious and priests.

The ethnic composition of those present at national meetings also changed. From the 1970s on, it was a struggle to give Hispanics, African-Americans, Asians, and other ethnic Catholics a prominent representation in liturgies and to use their native languages in more than a token way in prayer and worship. These new arrivals to the United States wanted to be heard. They clamored to hear speakers and read books in their own languages. They needed suitable catechetical materials, as did the English-speaking participants.

To address such challenges, in talks in Miami, Florida, and Raymondville, Texas, simultaneous translations were provided for catechists who did not speak or understand English. As I began my lecture in Raymondville, I heard people in the far back corner talking all through my presentation. At the break, a diocesan catechetical leader came to me to apologize. She had forgotten to tell me that there were seventy-five or so people in the back who knew no English but wanted to understand what was being said. So, in that session, bilingual catechists provided simultaneous translations of the materials presented.

In a small way, the increasing presence of Hispanic Catholics highlighted their struggles across the United States to be accepted in Catholic parishes and at national meetings. The Church lost many of them to evangelical churches because they did not feel welcomed by the Catholic community. They wanted to be understood, and they wanted to celebrate their faith in their native language.

Section 2:
MY CATECHETICAL JOURNEY

Interest in evangelization intensified in 1990, at about the time that my book on evangelization was published. My book was titled, *News That Is Good: Evangelization for Catholics.* The topics contained in this book became speaking points for my lectures. Archbishop Thomas Kelly of Louisville wrote me after a priests' convocation in December 1990. He said, "*News that is Good* is a treasured gift." After the Los Angeles Religious Education Congress on March 11, 1991, Archbishop Roger Mahoney sent me a letter saying that this book is a "valuable and important evangelical effort." In parishes and dioceses, my presentations focused on evangelization. Topics included: "Proclaiming God's Glory: Evangelization is the Heart of Ministry" and "Called to Proclaim in Our Culture" at the NCCE Convocation on June 15, 1990, in Houston.

With the Church's new focus on evangelization, Catholic evangelists, catechists, and pastoral ministers addressed the challenges from the secular world. The Toledo diocese recognized how this challenges families and invited me to speak on "A Vision of Church and Family" (March 9, 1990). In the same year, I spoke to the Wisconsin Directors of Religious Education Forum (WDREF) in Madison, Wisconsin, on "The Way of Jesus: Evangelizing and Catechizing" and "Practical Considerations for Ministry." This forum discussed the close connection between evangelization and catechesis. The theme of the gathering was "Evangelization: What's Missing in Catechesis?"

Gradually, religious educators nationwide grew in their appreciation of evangelization. The National Office for Persons with Disabilities recognized this at their Owensboro, Kentucky,

Conference on September 29, 1980. The reaction was the same at the Minneapolis Diocesan Convention on August 27-29, 1991. The theme at the Minneapolis convention was "Evangelization for Catholic Families, Church, and Parish." After I addressed evangelization at a Religious Education Assembly in Rapid City, South Dakota, Bishop Charles Chaput, OFM Cap, wrote me on March 21, 1991. He said: "So many people commented to me [about] how your presentations stirred their hearts. We are really grateful for this special ministry to us."

At that assembly, my talks were titled "The Way of Jesus: Evangelization and the Parish" and "Evangelization: Called to Proclaim in our Culture." On October 17, 1992, at the College of St. Rose in Albany, New York, the topic was, "Evangelization: What Is It?" Invitations to speak on evangelization included the OCEA Convention in Cincinnati (September 30–October 1, 1992), where the topic was "Evangelization in Catholic Schools." The NCCE Convention lecture in the same city on June 19-22, 1994, was titled "Holy Families are Evangelizing Families." The requested focus on evangelization continued as I responded in addresses on evangelization to priest convocations and religious and lay assemblies through the 1990s.

National and regional catechetical conferences included presentations on catechesis along with other Church ministries. The emergence of new ministries had a profound effect on parish and diocesan commitment to catechesis. Catechetical conferences often did not address catechesis in light of deeper issues confronting the Catholic Church. Those issues included the continuing secularization of this country and the worldly attitudes of its citizens. One effect of this secularization was the decline of Catholics who attended our churches. In the next generation, there was an even more radical drop in Sunday Mass attendance and the loss of Church members.

Catholic religious education conventions, large and small, chose topics that pertained to the needs of the time. They did a heroic job in the midst of the emergence of new ministries. They helped participants to gain knowledge about what was happening and helped them to grow in their particular ministries. Lectures and workshops addressed topics like liturgical catechesis, small Christian communities, Scripture, multicultural ministers, training for ministry, methodology, youth ministry, and adult education. These topics appeared in actual congress presentations.

Addresses at diocesan conventions and parishes followed similar themes. For example, I gave the following talks during that period: "Evangelization" (Chicago Catechetical Convention, 1992), "Proclaiming the Absolute Richness of Christ" (Fort Wayne [Indiana] Convention, 1993), "The *Catechism of the Catholic Church*: Celebrating the Gift" (Grand Rapids, Michigan, 1993), and the "Art of Collaboration in the Mission of the Church with Implications for Parish Life" (Little Rock [Arkansas] Priests' Convention, 1994).

The following responses to my presentations reflect the times. The first is from Sr. Jane Carew, who was diocesan catechetical director in Fort Wayne. She wrote: "Your address was incredibly well crafted to address the theme and implementation of our present structure. You put the *Catechism* in an excellent perspective, historically and catechetically. The address, while recognizing the validity of the new, emerging ministries, focused on the vital importance of catechesis in today's Church."

The second comment is from Bishop Andrew J. McDonald, then bishop of the Diocese of Little Rock. He wrote: "Our priests are most enthusiastic about the presentations which you have made concerning religious education and specifically the universal catechism. I join them in their enthusiasm."

The bishop's words indicate that it was becoming increasingly clearer that future catechesis had to move toward a more precise presentation of the essentials of the faith. The free-floating approach to catechetical formation, with heavy emphasis on experience and process, was fading. In its place came the recognition that it was vitally important to stress the fundamental beliefs of the faith.

To do this, it was necessary to acknowledge the powerful influence of the secular culture. To that end, organizers of the 1995 National Conference of Catechetical Leadership Convention asked me to reflect on the topic "What Should the Christian Response of Faith be in Light of our Culture and Creed?" The address focused on the power of culture, and its impact on catechesis and ministry.

As the second millennium came to an end, presentations specifically pertaining to catechesis and the new *Catechism* increased. This complemented the strong emphasis on the *Catechism of the Catholic Church* coming from the United States bishops. At the East Coast Conference for Religious Education in Washington in 1994, I spoke on "Today's Catechetical Challenge: Integrating Content and Methodology in Light of the *Catechism of the Catholic Church*." This attention to the catechism continued at the NCEA Convention in 1995. My address was titled "The Catechism: New Visions and New Directions." The same theme was reiterated in Lexington, Kentucky (1995), in Ogdensburg, New York (1996), and elsewhere.

While the *Catechism* was receiving more emphasis, there was a continuing need to energize catechists by reminding them of their roots in the life and mission of Jesus. The Lake Barkley Conference in Kentucky focused on "Jesus and Leadership" (1997). After speaking at the Pennsylvania Ministry Conference in Erie, Pennsylvania, the *Lake Shore Visitor* newspaper quoted me saying, "The need for spiritual renewal is the greatest need in the Church today" (September 10, 1999). My keynote address at the Las Vegas Religious Education Convention was titled "Walking on the Journey of Hope" (October 1999).

As the new millennium began, lectures in Albany, New York; Lexington, Kentucky; and at the Nebraska Festival of Faith centered on "Finding God in the Stories of Our Lives." Other themes included: rites of passage, family, and evangelization. At the Hofinger Conference (New Orleans, Louisiana, 2003) it was "The Catholic Family in a Changing World." I spoke at the National Conference for Catechetical Leadership (NCCL) annual conference on "Rites of Passage and the Journey of Faith" (2009), and at the CREDO Association of Religious Educators in Camden, New Jersey, on "Nurturing the Nurturers" (2012). Later, in 2013, I spoke at the MAREDA Retreat for Religious Educators in Milwaukee. My keynote topic was "Life's Transitions in a Living/Changing Church."

These titles give evidence that catechetical conferences across the country focused on more general topics and on motivational talks. These talks were meant to encourage and inspire the participants. There was a need to do more than simply stress basic Church teachings.

As this occurred on the national scene, there was no common pattern in catechesis in religious studies departments in universities, in parishes, and dioceses in the 1990s and in the early 2000s. In Catholic colleges and universities, academic attention to religious education and catechesis waned in the new millennium.

Before concluding this section, two points are worth mentioning.

1. New Church Ministries

The first point pertains to the vibrant development of numerous Church ministries, and the widespread discussion of them at national conferences, in dioceses, and in parishes. This helped the laity acknowledge their rightful place in Church ministry and governance. Pastoral ministry programs with a distinctive focus on lay ministry sprang up everywhere, and individual ministries were frequently featured at religious education congresses.

Despite all of this activity, the number of national seminars, workshops, and lectures on catechesis and teaching basic beliefs were inadequate. Many sessions focused on method and the catechetical process, but the content piece was not prominent. At one major religious education program held during the summer, featured lectures were on Christianity and capitalism, the faith of contemporary Christians, liturgical documents, and Christian families. These were timely topics. But, they did not answer the need for more instruction on teaching basic Catholic beliefs.

2. Knowledge of Faith Essentials

The second point that should be made deals with the actual knowledge of the essentials of the faith. Following the annual Religious Education Conference held in Boston, the November 2, 1990, issue of *The Pilot*, the archdiocesan newspaper, reported on my address "Catechesis: Framing Communities of Compassion." It quoted my cautions about Catholic theological illiteracy. *The Pilot* said, "Fr. Hater called upon catechists to teach our people solid, basic Catholic teaching, so that they can distinguish clearly what it means to be a Catholic Christian." This article from *The Pilot* implied that an interest in Catholic identity grew in significance at the turn of the new millennium.

University Teaching

Many catechists looked for fresh ways to get God's Word across to those they were trying to catechize. These professionals tried many things, but often minimal learning took place. It may sound harsh, but standing in front of undergraduate theology classes and trying to build upon student knowledge of the Catholic faith often produced little response. Theology professors often presumed that students had little prior knowledge of the basics of the faith.

When it came to graduate classes in religious education or theology, it was even more surprising how little some graduate students knew. This included both elementary school teachers of religion and catechists. They had only vague knowledge about matters of faith. This was due largely to the fact that there was no single source of knowledge once the *Baltimore Catechism* was no longer used. Instead, multiple sources of knowledge existed for them, and these sources did not always agree.

Graduate students, interested in teaching religion, were attracted by courses that presented good methodology and discussed ministry in general. There was far less interest in the didactic approach to catechesis. This began to change after the publication of the *Catechism of the Catholic Church*. As previously noted, the *Catechism* appeared at about the same time that the wave of traditional thinking emerged with undergraduate students and the Catholic population at large. This attachment to traditional Catholicism increased during the late 1990s.

Focus of National Conventions

Before the publication of the *Catechism of the Catholic Church*, dioceses and national conventions often brought in speakers to conduct workshops and give major addresses with no particular emphasis on the content of catechesis. These addressed ways to catechize or strategies for developing effective ministries. There was a strong focus on RCIA and its connection with liturgy and catechesis. Many other convention keynotes and lectures during these years focused on motivational issues. They dealt with spirituality, ministry, and adult faith formation.

Until the new millennium, no special approval from the local bishop was generally required to speak at these conventions. One benefit of not screening speakers was that attendees heard a pluriformity of views on ministerial and catechetical topics. The downside, of course, was the uncertainty it brought, especially when speakers disagreed on key issues. As lay ministers became common in parishes, the need arose to clarify what lay ministry meant for the average Catholic. After the sex abuse scandals, most bishops insisted on vetting all speakers coming from outside their dioceses.

As ministries proliferated, diocesan offices and parishes searched for solid approaches to catechesis. Perhaps they were hoping to find that magic key that would bring total success. Deep down, they knew that no magic key existed.

Conventions, catechetical meetings, university teaching, and parish ministry revealed similar issues. Everywhere, serious-minded diocesan, parish, and Catholic school leaders were committed to their mission. They wanted to effectively share the word and work of Jesus. Their efforts were a necessary preamble to the clarification that happened after the publication of the *Catechism of the Catholic Church.*

Over the years, more and more religious women and lay Catholics assumed leadership positions. They replaced priests at major catechetical conventions. Today, catechetical conventions are almost exclusively run and attended by lay Catholics. This change represents a significant emergence of lay ecclesial ministers. At a two-day retreat in May 2012 in Camden, New Jersey, all the participants — parish and diocesan religious education directors — were women.

Catechesis Improves

Before the 1990s, many bishops and priests did not exercise a strong supervisory role over catechesis. After a retreat centering on religious education for the priests of one diocese, the archbishop stood up and said: "During this retreat, I came to a clear insight about my ministry. In the future, I am going to take religious education in this diocese much more seriously." This he did. He later assumed a major national role in the implementation of the *Catechism of the Catholic Church.*

As salaried catechetical leaders grew in numbers, catechesis improved. At the same time, Catholic schools faced new challenges. There was a growing influx of non-Catholic students enrolling in the schools. There were also Catholic children whose parents were not Churchgoers, and Catholic school teachers who had received poor catechesis. The challenge for these schools was to maintain high standards and not water down basic Catholic teaching. This wasn't easy when the number of non-Catholics enrolled was growing. Concomitantly, with the emergence of Catholic mission schools, a high percentage of students were not Catholic. In these school situations, it was often a struggle for school principals and religion teachers who wished to teach the truths of the Catholic faith.

Dioceses emphasized better preparation and the certification of catechists. Coupled with this was the increased pressure exerted by the bishops' Subcommittee on the Catechism for catechists to be faithful to the language of the *Catechism*. Textbook writers and religion teachers continued to struggle with the challenge of helping students to understand the abstract language of the *Catechism*.

Textbook publishers, pastors, and catechetical leaders knew that what was taught must be taught in a way that students could understand. Otherwise, what was "learned" was no more than words. Words alone, even if they were memorized, had little effect on a student's life. The language used and the message taught must really communicate within the context of the times. The catechetical message must also remain faithful to what the Church teaches. This was not easy for catechists who had only a minimum of catechetical instruction.

As the requirements for catechesis tightened, strong traditional moments surfaced. Traditional Catholics often rejected previous catechetical procedures, opting instead for a traditional, monolithic approach to being Catholic. These traditionalists felt it was time to vigorously reassert Catholic beliefs. Many other Catholics felt that the new stress on traditionalism was an unfortunate overreaction.

The screening of catechetical speakers in dioceses and parishes and the growing emphasis on more traditional catechetical approaches became quite evident. The catechetical energy of the post-conciliar period faded away, and catechesis settled into a more regulated mode of action. Generally, catechetical programs followed the directives initiated by the *Catechism of the Catholic Church*. The *Catechism* and the *General Directory for Catechesis* became the primary resources and guides for parish catechesis as catechists, pastors, and catechetical leaders implemented their directives.

Paradoxically, as the catechetical enterprise grew stronger, paid parish directors of religious education (DREs) were often replaced by volunteer DREs. Many Parishes once hired professional DREs, often with master's degrees. But with tightening budgets, parishes often replaced the professional and paid DREs with volunteers who had previously worked as volunteer parish catechists.

This change weakened the overall quality of catechesis. Volunteer DREs often were not able to train volunteer catechists as effectively. They weren't as familiar with good catechetical materials. And these volunteer catechetical leaders were often not equipped to teach catechists solid catechetical content. These difficulties became clear in discussions at national conventions. I also heard these issues discussed when I was teaching at the university and working in parishes.

Parish attempts to catechize Catholics of all ages met with mixed results. It was harder to get people to attend catechetical sessions since fewer parents attended Mass on Sundays. It was difficult to get youths and young adults to continue their catechetical formation after they received the Sacrament of Confirmation and graduated from the eighth grade. In many ways, it was challenging to get the message across to the students.

Last Meeting with Cardinal Bernardin

My final communication with Cardinal Joseph Bernardin took place at the 1996 Chicago Catechetical Conference. He had been named the archbishop of Chicago in 1982 and become a cardinal in 1983. Cardinal Bernardin had invited me to give the conference keynote address: "Witness to Jesus Christ: Challenges in the Twenty-First Century." In 1995, the previous year, he had been diagnosed with pancreatic cancer.

I'll never forget his frail, tentative walk as he approached the front of the hall before he introduced me at the congress. When we shook hands, he was only a shadow of his former self. He was very pale and thin. As he struggled down the aisle from the back of the room, he carried the first religious education book that we had written together. We collaborated on it not long after I began the archdiocesan Office of Religious Education in Cincinnati.

During his introduction, he showed the book to the audience saying, "I wanted to call this book, *Let the Little Children Come to Me,* but Bob won out and we omitted the word little." Then, he described the beginnings of the Cincinnati religious education office.

In addition to inviting me to give this keynote address, the cardinal had also invited me to give a major address at the first national seminary conference, held at Mundelein Seminary in Chicago. That conference was to take place about a month after the catechetical congress.

When my congress address was over, Cardinal Bernardin and I spoke for quite a while. Before leaving me, he proudly gave me a revised version of our original book. The revised book, written and adapted by the Chicago Office of Religious Education, gave us credit for our original work. Before this revision began in Chicago, the cardinal had asked Rev. John Pollard, the director of the Chicago office to contact me.

My friend and I spoke of old times in Cincinnati. When it was time to go, the cardinal said: "Bob, you gave a great talk today. I'll see you next month at the seminary conference at Mundelein Seminary." He needed to meet other participants but was in no hurry. Eventually, we walked out of the convention area together. As he labored to go to the next venue, he greeted many people, always smiling and offering his prayers and best wishes.

When we said goodbye, I watched him walk away, greet convention attendees, and disappear into the crowd. The cardinal's stooped shoulders and slow shuffle seemed to symbolize the struggle he experienced during the forty years of his priesthood. He died soon afterward, on November 14, 1996.

A month later, I was back in Chicago to participate in the first annual Mundelein Seminary Convention. While there, the seminary rector showed me the late cardinal's room and office. He pointed to his desk, and the only thing left on the desk — Cardinal Bernardin's reading glasses. It was the only item on a desk once filled with important papers. Sensing the presence of my longtime friend and colleague, I said quietly: "Thanks, Joe, for your friendship, and for getting me involved in religious education. It has been an interesting journey."

In retrospect, the challenges Cardinal Bernardin dealt with in catechesis were significant. When he showed the Chicago conference our first book written in the early 1970s and then gave me the new Chicago edition of the same book, I realized that these two books marked the beginning and end of an era of catechesis. The present one was ending, and a new era was beginning. New directions were emerging. These signaled a continued clarification of the catechetical enterprise in the twenty-first century.

Section 3:
TRENDS AND CONCLUSIONS FROM THIS PERIOD

With directives coming from the Subcommittee on the Catechism, book publishers, pastors, diocesan and parish catechetical leaders, and catechists all emphasized the teaching of the content of the Catholic faith. Gradual solidification occurred as catechetical leaders devised ways to teach the fundamentals of the faith in ways that related to the experience of the catechized. This effort continued through the first decades of the twenty-first century.

In 2004, I wrote an article that appeared in the *Catechetical Leader*, a professional magazine that was published by the National Conference for Catechetical Leadership. My article, "Advancing Excellence in Catechetical Ministry," listed catechetical needs of that time. It appears in an edited version in this section. The needs coming from this period were:

1. Take seriously the cultural context when doing catechetical ministry.

Secular culture is the greatest challenge that catechists face. They have to accommodate their catechesis to life's fast pace, society's materialism, cultural relativism, and rampant immorality. Catechesis must be sensitive to diverse family situations, pressures on adults, and the various ethnic cultures in every parish.

When addressing cultural issues, catechists should keep in mind that the world is basically good, but wounded. God is always present at the heart of society. With this in mind, Church ministers can and should employ any modern technological tools at their disposal that can further the cause of the Gospel (*GDC*, 20).

2. Consider a person's complete experience and life situation, especially as regards family and work, while presenting the basic teachings of the Church.

The *GDC* emphasizes being sensitive to people's actual conditions. Jesus did this; so must catechists in the secular world they face. As He taught the crowds, He reached out to all kinds of poor people. Catechesis must be adapted to the person's vocabulary, times, and culture (194).

The family is central in the catechist's ministry. The home is the foundation for faith in the midst of worldly pressures. Social changes affect the domestic Church. The stress on materialism, the pressures of work, and the involvement of children in too many secular activities all weaken the religious fabric of the home.

The *GDC* reiterates that parents are the primary educators of their children (226). Often, one parent, grandparent, or a guardian raises the children. Values assimilated from the home environment affect the child's participation in parish catechetical activities. Divorce, job loss, terrorist threats, and sickness also affect families, and children often suffer the consequences. Catechesis needs to account for such challenges and adapt the

Christian message to the needs of the times. In so doing, catechists must be flexible, and catechetical programs and teaching need to address divergent factors that face today's Catholics.

3. Teach basic Catholic beliefs (content) using solid catechetical approaches.

While stressing the need to teach the basics of the faith in a systematic and comprehensive way, the *GDC* emphasized that full faith formation requires solid content and method. The goal of catechesis is conversion which leads to active living of the Christian life, modeled on Christ (149). Hence, catechesis must include every aspect of educating and bringing the disciple into oneness with the Lord. In this effort, strong emphasis is given to developing a love and knowledge of the Scriptures as the Word of God.

Information and formation are essential components of catechesis. To achieve ongoing faith formation, contemporary catechesis must employ a variety of approaches that connect the Word of God with the cultural and personal experiences of the catechized. (*GDC*, 148).

When discussing the teaching of religion in Catholic schools, the *GDC* distinguished between catechesis and religious instruction (73). In Catholic schools, religious instruction sets the stage or prepares students for life by introducing them to Catholic beliefs and values. Such instruction has an evangelizing character. Christian disciples use these values and beliefs to challenge the values of secular culture. Religious instruction must relate to other areas of knowledge. Consequently, it is a scholastic discipline and should be pursued with rigor and professionalism (73).

Because it focuses on the content of the faith, the *Catechism of the Catholic Church* is the main reference and source for catechists. Catechists should stress fundamental aspects of Church teaching, such as Scripture, the Trinity, Incarnation, redemption, salvation, sin, grace, the Mass, sacraments, and morality. These should be taught according to the ability of the catechized. This may require memorization, but equally as important is the ability of the learner to apply what is taught to life.

4. Recognize that storytelling and sharing personal faith stories are significant aspects of catechesis, especially biblical catechesis.

The secularity of the third millennium leaves a vacuum in peoples' souls. Catholics are often hungry for Scripture, which is basic to all catechesis. All catechesis depends on the Word of God as it is interpreted in the Church's sacred Tradition.

Today's catechists are to imitate Jesus, the greatest catechist of all. He showed the way, by taking people where they were — Zacchaeus, the woman at the well, the woman caught in adultery. He addressed them in light of God's Word. He taught through parables and stories, thus enabling His listeners to connect His teachings with their Hebrew traditions and personal lives.

Catholics can be taught to better understand Scripture. The catechist must do this by giving children, youths, and adults an appreciation of the biblical texts. Catechesis must also teach about Jesus, Mary the Mother of God, Peter, Mary Magdalene, Paul, and others in a way that the catechized can see them as role models. Catechists teach the catechized how specific parts of Scripture relate to Church teachings, the sacraments, the Mass, social justice, and how they apply to life.

5. Employ different catechetical approaches, including various initiatory approaches. See GDC, 69-71.

After the experiential focus of the 1970s and 1980s, catechetical leaders realized that no one method suffices. People differ, and since conversion is ongoing various approaches are necessary at various stages of faith formation. The Word of God must be adapted to personal and social contexts. The *GDC* refers to the gradual revelatory process as the "principle of the progressiveness of Revelation" (143).

6. Recognize catechetical ministry as an aspect of the new evangelization.

How can we stop the loss of Catholics from our faith and how can we bring back those who left? Popes John Paul II, Benedict XVI, and Francis have all addressed this question. This lessening of commitment to the Catholic Church has inspired recent popes to call for a new evangelization that is both missionary and pastoral.

The pastoral component of the New Evangelization strives to bring back to the Church those who left. It uses catechesis as a tool. The 2012 world Synod of Bishops treated many aspects of evangelization and mission, including catechesis and effective ways to present the Word of God to younger generations. A vital part of the New Evangelization is to catechize effectively.

As the numbers of Catholics attending Sunday Mass continues to decline, some who left the Church go to evangelical mega-churches. Others attend churches belonging to other denominations. Still others drop out and attend no church at all. To encourage former Catholics to return to the Church is a great challenge. This must begin by making those who return feel welcome. What good is it to ask them to return if nothing has changed? How long will they stay if they find the parishes are no different from when they left?

Seeing catechesis as an aspect of evangelization has profound consequences for catechesis (*Catechesi Tradendae*, 18; *GDC*, 63). Even though Pope John Paul II set the direction by rooting catechesis in the evangelization process in the 1970s, it was not until after the publication of the *GDC* that the implications of this approach became clear to catechetical leaders. Evangelization is the driving force, or the heart of catechesis. Evangelization recognizes the depths of God's love in the Paschal Mystery. It sees happiness in the kingdom of God as its final goal.

The Church's mission is closely related to its task of evangelization. Evangelization motivates Christian disciples to reach out to those who do not know Christ, or to those whose faith has become weak (missionary). In the Christian community, catechists introduce neophytes into the mystery of Christ and help them complete their initiation (initiatory). And catechists continue to initiate the Christian faithful into the mystery of Christ in the midst of the community (pastoral) (*GDC*, 49).

For catechesis to be effective and truly evangelizing, catechists must focus their teaching, ministry, and policies in light of a worldview that centers on social awareness, scientific breakthroughs, technological advances, and the concern for all peoples.

7. Recognize that catechesis is lifelong, beginning at birth, and lasting until death.

Catechizing on the essentials of the faith establishes a necessary foundation for growth in the whole Christian life. The *GDC* stressed the right of every baptized person to receive such solid catechesis (167). This right applies to young children, youths, active adults, and elderly people. It is true for children in Catholic schools and those in public schools. It applies to physically, emotionally, and mentally challenged persons. The responsibility of the Christian community to provide adequate catechesis extends to people from birth to death.

Ongoing faith formation is sensitive to people's conditions, including the environment where they live. Hence, catechesis often differs in urban and rural settings, and in different ethnic populations. When environments change, catechesis needs to develop a new focus as catechists look to the Church for stability, support, and authentic Catholic belief.

8. Place high priority on adult faith formation while not neglecting children and youth catechesis.

Since Vatican II, Church documents give priority to adult faith formation, modeled on the Rite of Christian Initiation of Adults. This rite takes into account the ways adults learn. Many adults are at different faith levels. Some manifest deep faith, others have never been fully catechized, and still others left the practice of their faith. In each situation, the person is at a different point.

Effective adult catechesis listens to people's stories and helps them to identify key times when God was with them on their faith journey. Catechists must be sensitive to ordinary life experiences that elicit a faith response. This is true especially at the time of baptisms, marriages, and funerals. But, there can be other crucial times or events as well. These occasions are opportunities to help adults open up and better appreciate God's presence in their lives (*GDC*, 176).

Catechesis keeps in mind the spiritual need of older adults, especially frail and dying people. The Christian community includes the elderly, asks for their wisdom, and invites them to participate in its faith life (*GDC*, 186). When a community of faith recognizes the treasure of its elderly, it grows in appreciation of God's love.

While stressing adult faith formation, the *GDC* reiterates the importance of excellent children's and youth catechesis (177-184). Young people need family and parish support to appreciate the Christian message. Youths are special targets of our secular culture. They can easily lose hope for a meaningful future when they witness greed, violence, and immorality on television, the Internet, and among adults and friends. They need role models that a committed Christian community can provide (*GDC*, 181).

9. Recognize the importance of the bishop and pastor in catechetical ministry.

The U.S. bishops took leadership in supporting the development of a universal catechism. The publication of the *Catechism of the Catholic Church* was an important step in the revitalization of catechesis. The *General Directory for Catechesis* was another.

The *GDC* acknowledges the bishop's responsibilities for catechesis. It refers to Vatican II documents that describe the chief duties of the bishops. It stresses that among those responsible for catechesis, the bishop is the one with the most responsibility. While calling on catechetical ministers to assist him, he alone has the final responsibility (222).

The *GDC*, citing *Catechesi Tradendae*, calls upon the bishop to give priority to catechetical ministry. He should be vigilant about it, stress catechist preparation, and oversee diocesan catechetical programs. The pastor is the bishop's chief representative in the parish. Pastors are responsible to call forth catechetical leaders and catechists. They must provide adequate formation for them and supervise the parish's catechetical enterprise.

The pastor sets the tone for parish catechesis. He establishes its fundamental orientation, supports catechetical ministers, and promotes the catechist's vocation. Pastors should use the *Catechism of the Catholic Church* as a reference book. It gives them the opportunity to refocus catechesis, but it will be only as effective as the Church's ability to cope with basic Church issues today.

The sex abuse scandal that involved some priests, and the shadowy way it was sometimes handled, continues to impede the effectiveness of bishops and pastors. This caused tremendous pain and scandal in the Catholic community. It brought about defections from the Church, and resulted in untold hurt among the victims. This issue came to the attention of the Catholic population late in the twentieth century. It seriously diminished the authority of the bishops and priests, and impacted the attitudes many people had toward Church leaders. This means that today's bishops and priests have to make even greater efforts to regain the trust of Catholics. Without this trust, the catechized will find it difficult to follow teachings they were taught.

10. Realize that parishes require the living witness of competent catechists, catechetical leaders, pastors, and catechetical communities.

It goes without saying that catechists have to know what they are talking about. They must also take the time to prepare their lessons well. It's not sufficient to walk into a catechetical session unprepared and then simply go through the textbook with the students. More is required. In saying this, we should remember that the person of the catechist is part of the teaching. The witness of the teacher is more important than the content taught, or the approach used. Regardless of a person's exemplary Catholic life, no catechist can effectively catechize without knowing what is taught and teaching it effectively.

Jesus is present among us through the living witness of His Church community and through Scripture. The *GDC* stresses that catechists must be living witnesses Christ's presence. Because of their ministry, special charisms are given to catechists (156).

The Holy Spirit, present in the catechist, moves the person to a deeper spirituality. This spirituality reaches expression in the living witness of faith. This is a more powerful testimony to the risen Lord than any catechetical book. It gives credence to the formal contents of catechesis.

The catechist needs the support of the Christian community. The catechized see the living Word actualized through the witness of loving parish members (*GDC*, 158). In the RCIA, initiation into the Christian life takes place in the midst of the community. This invites catechetical leaders to inspire, motivate, and coordinate the parish's ministry of the Word.

11. Realize the close link between catechesis and other pastoral ministries, especially liturgy and the social justice dimension of the Gospels.

As an aspect of evangelization, catechesis relates to other forms of evangelization, especially service ministries, and liturgy. Besides the liturgical focus present in catechetical activities, catechesis recognizes the significance of relating more closely with specific liturgical activities, especially the sacraments (*GDC*, 51).

The RCIA shows the intimate connection between catechesis and liturgy. Catechesis focuses on Jesus' call to proclaim the kingdom of God, to work for justice, and to stir Christian hearts and minds to minister to hurting and poor people (*GDC*, 17). When Jesus began His public ministry, He proclaimed a message of hope for the poor and disenfranchised. In so doing, He established a kingdom for all people (*GDC*, 163). The community celebrates this hope in the liturgy.

12. Include ecumenical and interreligious dimensions in catechesis, when appropriate.

As interfaith marriages increased, catechists recognized the importance of taking this into account as they catechized. Catechists are to be especially sensitive to families where some members are not Catholic. With growing numbers of non-Christian peoples in neighborhoods and workplaces, Catholics need to develop a better appreciation of their faith in an interreligious context.

The *GDC* mentions the ecumenical dimension of catechetical ministry (197). It calls for an ecumenical focus for catechesis, and encourages parishes to participate in ecumenical activities (*GDC*, 197). Catechists need to know their faith, recognize similarities and differences between different faith traditions, and emphasize the unity of faith. When catechizing, catechists must make clear the uniqueness of the Catholic faith.

The Catholic community yearns for solid catechesis. The catechetical tools are now in place for this to happen. Good catechetical materials and textbooks are available. More is required, however, than just the desire for solid catechesis and good catechetical materials. Effective catechesis is a matter of the heart. It requires sacrifice and the setting of priorities on the part of parents, catechists, and parishes. The Catholic community is invited to follow the Spirit's lead and put its ministry under the patronage of Mary, the Mother of God. Just as she brought forth Jesus, now she will ask her Son to bring forth life in the parish through dedicated catechetical ministers.

CHAPTER 6

INCARNATIONAL CATECHESIS IN A CONTEMPORARY CONTEXT

"For a catechist, beginning with Christ first means to 'stay with their Teacher, listen to him and learn from him.'"

(Pope Francis, *Address to International Catechetical Congress*, September 27, 2013)

Previous chapters analyzed the trends in catechesis during the past sixty years. This chapter anticipates the future by analyzing incarnational theology as it relates to the contemporary social and ecclesial context. This analysis is the basis for this book, *Common Sense Catechesis*.

The Catholic faith is a sacramental faith. We see glimpses of God in nature, creation, and good people. In a sense, creation is God's first incarnation. Acknowledging God's presence in nature sets the stage for His revelation in the Old and New Testaments. Jesus is the fullest expression of who God is. He assumed flesh in the womb of Mary at the Incarnation.

We probe new catechetical directions by focusing on the centrality of the Incarnation. This chapter, which stresses the importance of establishing a solid theological basis for catechesis, is divided into three sections. Section 1 considers incarnational catechesis. Section 2 looks at our secular environment as the place where the Christian catechist ministers. Section 3 presents the guidelines provided by the U.S. Catholic bishops through their Subcommittee on the Catechism.

Section 1:
THE CENTRALITY OF THE INCARNATION IN CATECHESIS

Vatican II brought about a shift in theology. Prior to the council, while recognizing Jesus' role in God's plan of salvation, the Latin, or Western, Catholic Church focused strongly on God the Father. The Eastern Church stressed the role of the Holy Spirit in the economy of salvation. Vatican II shed fresh insights on Jesus' role in God's universal plan.

In a new way, the council's teaching affirmed the vital role of Jesus in Church life, ministry, and scholarship. The Incarnation of the Son of God is the central event of all history, revealing God's love in a new way. This revelation was brought to fruition in Jesus' death and resurrection. His death points to the evil of sin and shows us the wonder of our all-loving Creator.

Church documents after Vatican II reiterate the centrality of the Incarnation in catechetical efforts. They stress that Jesus is the Good News *(Evangelii Nuntiandi*, 7), and that catechesis is a "pedagogy of the incarnation" (*GDC*, 143). They show Jesus as the most perfect incarnation of God's love.

References are made to God's revelation in certain key passages. "In the beginning was the Word, and the Word was with

God, and the Word was God.... All things came to be through him, and without him no thing came to be" (Jn 1:1-3). After the fall of Adam and Eve, divine love poured itself out into a blessed yet fallen world. God's promise of a savior in the Hebrew Scriptures was climaxed in Jesus' incarnation, life, death, and resurrection.

The role of catechesis was made clearer with the publication of the following documents: *Evangelii Nuntiandi (EN), Catechesi Tradendae (CT), the General Directory for Catechesis (GDC),* and the *National Directory for Catechesis (NDC). Evangelii Nuntiandi* stresses that evangelization is the "vocation proper to the Church, her deepest identity" (14). *Catechesi Tradendae* indicates that catechesis is a central aspect of the "rich, complex, and dynamic reality of evangelization" (18). These documents say that the chief content of catechesis is the person and message of Jesus. They also discuss the multidimensional approach used by Jesus in proclaiming the Word of God.

The *NDC* summarizes different forms of catechesis, including the initial proclamation of the Gospel, biblical catechesis, doctrinal catechesis, moral catechesis, liturgical catechesis, and sacramental catechesis (p. 86). When considering various ways to share the mystery of God's love, the question arises, "Is there a fundamental perspective that underlies all of them?" Hints at an answer to this question can be gleaned by reflecting on Pope Benedict XVI's encyclical *Deus Caritas Est (God Is Love).*

Catechetical insights derived from his words suggest an orientation for all catechesis. We describe this as "Incarnational Catechesis." We can see it as the fundamental perspective for all catechesis. It puts Christ at the center.

God: Incarnated in Jesus

Jesus was sent by the Father to save us (see Jn 6:38-39). The unique incarnation of the Son of God, the Word made Flesh, is a sign of God's love. Jesus carries out the mission that His Father gave Him — namely, the salvation of humankind, through His life, actions, and words. His mission climaxed on the cross, and He was raised up by the Father as the eternal sign of divine sonship and God's love.

Deus Caritas Est provides theological insights used by incarnational catechesis. In the section of the encyclical entitled "Jesus Christ — the Incarnate Love of God," Pope Benedict explains what he means. He says that the real originality of the New Testament is found not so much in new ideas but "in the figure of Christ himself, who gives flesh and blood to these concepts — an unprecedented realism" (12).

Pope Benedict expands on this statement by using parables — for example, the shepherd — to make a central point. He says, "These are no mere words: they constitute an explanation of his very being and activity." Jesus' being is the main focus. In other words, His basic nature is to shepherd, to forgive, and to be anything else that the parables disclose.

The pope specifically refers to the Parable of the Good Shepherd. He indicates that Jesus is a shepherd in His very being. His nature is to be a shepherd, with all this entails. Jesus is attentive to His sheep. He seeks out strays. He never gives up on them.

Jesus also reveals His nature as a forgiving God in the story of the adulterous woman. It is Jesus' nature to forgive. Even as others condemned her, He forgives the woman and tells her to sin no more. When we sin, Jesus stands at our side because He loves us and never abandons us.

The parables revealing who Jesus is climax in the account of His crucifixion. He accepts this gruesome death because He is God. The same Word who moved over the waters in creation hangs thirsting for water because He is God. This is love incarnate. The ultimate expression of God's love is revealed only in Jesus' story.

The pope refers to Jesus' death as the climax of God's love "in its most radical form" (*Deus Caritas Est*, 12). Meditating on the radical nature of God's love, revealed in Jesus' crucifixion, is the starting point of *God Is Love*.

The pope next focuses on the enduring presence of Christ's act of oblation, as manifested in the Eucharist. Jesus is the "ultimate logos." This logos "becomes food for us — as love. The Eucharist draws us into Jesus' self-oblation ... as we enter into the very dynamic of his self-giving" (13). Christians now share "in his body and blood" (13).

The pope points to the communal nature of Holy Communion, for by it we "become one with the Lord, like all the other communicants" (14). He continues, saying, "Communion draws me out of myself towards him, and thus towards unity with all Christians" (15). In so doing, "we become 'one body' completely joined in a single existence" (15).

All Christians who participate in the Eucharist are commissioned to carry on the mission that Christ initiated. Since they are members of His Body, they are to serve as shepherds, teachers, forgivers of sins, and prophets.

Risen Christ: Incarnated in the Church's Story

The unity of all communicants at the Eucharist creates a communal context and is the perfect expression of the Church as the Body of Christ. For the sake of this unity, the Word of God must be included in all Church ministry, especially in catechesis and liturgy.

Insights gleaned from *Deus Caritas Est* put into focus the significance of story. During Jesus' time, His life and teachings incarnated the Father's designs. After the Resurrection and Pentecost, His presence continues in the lives and actions of believing Christians through the power of the Holy Spirit. The stories of Christians reflect Jesus' ongoing Incarnation in their lives. Stories, describing the lives of Mary, the saints, and holy people also illustrate this connection between faith and life.

The New Testament reveals the story of Jesus' incarnation. The Church's story and the stories of Christians manifest the continuing presence of the incarnate Lord. In this sense, their stories are Jesus stories, as the risen Lord continues to live through them. Even though God is present in nature, the most perfect expression of His divine presence is found in Jesus and the Christian story. Thus the story is a fruitful ground for proclaiming the catechetical message.

The same Lord who hung on the cross to reveal God's love pours himself out through the lives of faithful Christians. One of those faithful Christians is Fr. Bill. His story and the story of every other faithful Christian manifest Jesus' incarnate presence:

> One hot summer afternoon, Bill, a seminarian, dug a grave at his religious community's headquarters for a missionary who suffered martyrdom in a far-off land. He was a year from ordination. As Bill worked, he thought: "Lord, each missionary must be prepared to accept death as one's ultimate fate. I must be prepared to take up my cross, ready to die for what I believe."

After ordination, Fr. Bill was sent to China as a missionary. After he arrived in 1939, the Japanese air force began bombing his village. Eventually, he fled with some parishioners into the mountains. No one heard from him for about a year. One day, word arrived that he was in a dingy lockup in India. Bill suffered a serious mental breakdown. Eventually, he returned to the United States, but never fully recovered. He spent the next fifty years doing menial tasks for his religious community.

Twenty years after coming home, his brother received a call from a pawn shop operator in Boston. He said that someone pawned a priest's chalice with Fr. Bill's name on it. How it got from China to this shop, no one knows. It was eventually returned to Fr. Bill who used it until his death. This chalice came to be known as the "resurrection chalice," symbolic of a missionary's sacrifice and his faithfulness until his death.

At Fr. Bill's funeral Mass, years later, his family and religious community wondered why many ordinary, unknown people from the neighboring town attended his funeral. This priest, considered as incapable of doing full priestly ministry because of his condition, spent years celebrating Mass, saying the Rosary, walking through the city, and getting to know other broken, vulnerable people. He became their spiritual adviser.

Little did Fr. Bill realize when he stood at the missionary's grave before his ordination that his cross and death would not be a bodily one, but a mental one. That cross lasted the rest of his life. His deep faith led Fr. Bill to a mysticism and commitment that few people experience. His holiness, won by accepting his cross, became a source of blessing for many ordinary people he met along life's path.

Jesus' life, suffering, death, and resurrection are central to our faith. His presence in His risen body, in the Church, and in the Eucharist are rooted in the mystery of the Incarnation. They were manifested in Fr. Bill's life, and are disclosed in the life of every faithful Christian. The risen Lord worked through Fr. Bill's brokenness in a way that he never envisioned. This priest's life gives testimony to the dying and rising of Jesus that continues in the body of Christians, especially in the poor and disenfranchised.

Incarnational Catechesis: Theological Perspectives and Responses

Incarnational catechesis involves sharing God's Word in light of Jesus' incarnation which continues in the Christian community. Incarnational catechesis' starting point from the theological perspectives contained in Pope Benedict XVI's *Deus Caritas Est*, and it grounds all catechetical efforts.

The fruits of Jesus' incarnation extended through His life and beyond. For the sake of clarification, the major events in Jesus' life are listed in the following schema. A theological theme and suggested personal responses accompany each event. The theological themes are gleaned from reflecting on the encyclical. The Suggested Responses offer suggestions for catechists as they consider the events from Jesus' life and the Theological Themes.

Jesus' Life Event	Theological Theme	Suggested Responses
Incarnation	Jesus' Being or Nature	Faith – Gratitude (God with Us)
Last Supper	Eucharist	Wonder – Appreciation (Ongoing Presence)
Crucifixion	Love Poured Out	Conviction – Love in Sacrifice (This is the Son of God)
Resurrection	Presence	Conversion – Hope (Change)
Pentecost	Body of Christ – The Church	Commitment – Church Mission (Service)

The ongoing dynamic of Jesus' incarnation is the foundation of incarnational catechesis. Jesus' Life Events and the Theological Themes are the pillars for all catechetical methods. Catechists are to give priority to these basic Catholic beliefs. They must also allow these beliefs to enter into dialogue with the presence of the incarnate God in the activities of faithful Christians and in the secular world where they live and work.

Catechetical Perspectives

The Paschal Mystery reveals God's incarnate love. Catechists give it flesh and life through their Christian witness. The following catechetical perspectives invite their response.

- **Focus on the being or nature of Jesus.**

  This helps catechists reflect on the importance of becoming "other Christs." They are to concentrate on Christ as a "subject," by reflecting on the awe-inspiring truth that this man of flesh and blood who walked the earth is also the Son of God. He is true God and true man, like us in all things, except sin.

  In witnessing to this teaching about Christ, catechists can see themselves as other Christs in who they are and what they do. They recognize who they are in their very being. Jesus lives and ministers through them. This is the basic starting point of incarnational catechesis. It is always relational and operates on the firm faith that the incarnate, risen Lord is present in any relationship rooted in divine love.

  To maintain this faith perspective, spiritual formation is vital for catechists. It invites catechetical leaders to plan retreats and days of prayer to help catechists better recognize themselves and other Christians as other Christs. This spiritual orientation sets the groundwork for how catechists teach.

- **See the Crucifixion as the culmination of divine love.**

  Every Christian of deep faith recognizes this truth. It helps catechists acknowledge the role of Jesus' crucifixion in God's plan of salvation. It helps them recognize the need to suffer in union with Christ. It also helps them witness by word and example that Jesus' dying and rising continues through the joys and sorrows of life.

- **Acknowledge Jesus' resurrection as the reason and cause of Christian hope.**

  Without the Resurrection, our faith would be in vain. In this world, often beset with gloom, disappointment, fear, and hopelessness, the catechist reminds the catechized that Jesus continues to live among us. The resurrection of Jesus is the ground of our hope. His suffering and death serve an eternal purpose. Jesus redeemed the human race from the sin of Adam and Eve, and from all subsequent sins committed by the human race.

- **Focus catechetical ministry on Jesus' presence in the Church and the sacraments.**

  The Church is the Body of Christ and the People of God. Jesus' incarnation in the Christian community reminds us that His ever-present love will never be far from those who seek it. No matter what our past lives have been, the risen Lord brings hope into the hearts of those who have no hope.

- **Connect Jesus' radical love on the cross with His on-going presence in the Church, the Eucharist, and the world.**

  This requires an appreciation of God's presence in life, and a firm belief in the centrality of the Mass as Jesus' ongoing sacrifice for sin. The suffering and death of Jesus is the supreme act of God's love for us. The Eucharist celebrates our connection with the entire Church, the Body of Christ. It also reminds us of our responsibility to continue Christ's mission of service.

Fr. Bill's chalice, symbolizing his own life of suffering, is a powerful reminder that every Christian must take up the cross to follow Christ. Catechists explain this belief by living it themselves, serving others, and using good catechetical methods.

- **Recognize that all faithful Christians live as other Christs, in union with each other as the Body of Christ.**

  This catechetical perspective puts the resurrection of Jesus in a new light. As Fr. Bill walked the streets ministering to ordinary people, he must have realized this. So does every disciple who sees the face of Christ in the needy and poor. This becomes more real when catechists realize that Jesus lives through their lives and ministry.

- **"Find Christ in the peripheries."**

  This favorite expression of Pope Francis reminds Christians of their responsibility to reach out to the needy and poor, regardless of the kind of poverty they experience. This Catholic social justice message is at the heart of the Gospel. It continually reminds us of the risen Lord. He is active and alive, and with those who need Him and receive His eternal love.

- **Challenge catechists to incorporate the catechetical message into appropriate cultural contexts.**

  This catechetical perspective leads to "common sense catechesis." The Pentecost experience led the early Christian community to proclaim the message of Jesus as Fr. Bill did on his walks through the city. This is also the Holy Spirit's invitation to every Christian.

The need to inculturate Jesus' message invites catechists to proclaim God's Word so that it is understood and appreciated. Catechists are to stress Scripture, teach the basic beliefs of the Catholic faith, and use appropriate catechetical methods. The spirit of the risen Lord lives in all peoples and nations. Pope John Paul II spoke about this in 1984, at the National Shrine to the Canadian Martyrs in Midland, Ontario.

> Thus the one faith is expressed in different ways. There can be no question of adulteration [of] the word of God or of emptying the Cross of its power, but rather of Christ animating the very center of all cultures. Thus, not only is Christianity relevant to the Indian peoples, but Christ, in the members of his body, is himself *Indian*. (Achiel Peelman, *Christ Is a Native American*, Orbis Books, Maryknoll, New York, 1995, p. 13)

This profound statement applies to everyone who catechizes and is catechized.

- **Root incarnational theology in the Trinity.**

When it comes to catechesis, it is imperative that whatever is taught or written teaches about Jesus' union with the Father and the Holy Spirit. In stressing Jesus' love for us, manifested especially on the cross, we remind the catechized that Jesus' love is a reflection of the Father's love.

It is also a revelation of how the Trinity pours out this love on humankind through the intercession of the Holy Spirit, the spirit of love. The catechist incarnates this love when acting in God's name and proclaiming the divine message of eternal love.

To summarize, the divine Word of God was incarnated in human flesh in Jesus. We learned about the Trinity and God's love for us through the revelation of the Word. The Word is the second person of the Trinity who became flesh. Applied to catechesis, this means that the divine Word of God revealed in the life and teachings of Jesus continues to live in our world. It is incarnated in the Church, her ministry, and in the lives of faithful Christians.

As far as the catechist is concerned, this means that whenever a catechist teaches the Word of God, it must be connected in some way with the Church and with the lives of the catechized. The Word must also be incarnated within them, so that they can understand it and see its ramifications. This, in a nutshell, is incarnational catechesis. It is the foundation for common sense catechesis.

The Word became flesh two thousand years ago, and Jesus continues to enflesh His love in His body, the Church. Because of God's love, the Word still becomes flesh today. This is a great source of Christian hope.

Section 2:
THE SECULAR ARENA CHALLENGES CATECHESIS

When looking at the past sixty years of catechesis, I related catechesis to the social and Church trends of the times. Now, we ask, "How can this historical analysis help us to take a new look at catechesis and provide a window into the future?"

Analysis of the post-Vatican II world set the stage for considering the needs of contemporary Catholics. These needs include meaning, intimacy, community, roots, fulfillment beyond the functional, certitude, and credible authority. In addressing them, incarnational catechesis helps us see that the Word of God contains answers to the alienation in today's world.

We all search for meaning in our busy lives. What does life mean to a child whose family is torn apart by divorce, abuse, or drugs? What does it mean to an adult whose work involves putting computerized parts into an impersonal system? To a college graduate who, after spending $110,000 for an education, cannot find work? To an eighty-year-old man without family or friends who lives in a nursing home?

The secular environment invites catechists to help the catechized realize that ultimate meaning is found only in God. The incarnate God of heaven and earth is present in a real sacramental way in their everyday lives. They are invited to form a personal relationship with Him.

In his homily at Mass on the Day of the Catechists in Rome, on September 29, 2013, Pope Francis addressed people's searching for meaning in secular things. He said:

> How do some people, perhaps ourselves included, end up becoming self-absorbed and finding security in material things which ultimately rob us of our face, our human face? This is what happens when we become complacent, when we no longer remember God.... When we no longer remember God, we too

become unreal, we become empty; like the rich man
in the Gospel, we no longer have a face!

To address secular society's replacement of spiritual values
with materialistic concern, we reflect on life's ultimate purpose. In
this context, the *Catechism of the Catholic Church* offers probing
questions to be incorporated into a catechetical session. It says:

Where do we come from and where are we going?
What is our beginning and what is our end? Where
does everything come from and where is it going?
Two questions, the first about the origins and the
second about ends, are inseparable and decisive for
the meaning and orientation of our life and behavior.
(282)

Catechists must continually relate the catechetical message to the situations of the catechized. They should constantly
point out that the incarnate God dwells in the midst of what
seems to be a godless society. This might mean encouraging
children to put out an elderly neighbor's garbage each week
without pay as an act of charity. Catechists can point to this
kind action as a reflection of Jesus ministering to the needy.
For adolescents, it could mean learning to refuse to go along
with the social pressure that promotes premarital sex when
their peers think it is okay. For adults, it might mean taking
a job that pays less money to be home more often with their
families. In each case, the catechists can help people look to the
scriptures for answers that are not available in a secular context.

Today's people are hungry for intimacy in an impersonal
world. Youths and young adults often reflect on their needs

for intimacy. Some substitute sex, drinking, and drugs for intimacy. A young woman' remarked: "I really don't enjoy sex that much. I'd rather be friends, but I feel so lonely. Sex helps me overcome this feeling, but it never lasts. Most of my friends do it, but there has to be a better way." Some adults turn to illicit or extra-marital sexual encounters when they are lonely or fail to find satisfaction in their fast-paced world and in their marriages.

Incarnational catechesis teaches us that fulfilling intimacy needs, while necessary, must be done in appropriate and moral ways. This means that human intimacy must be regulated by Christian moral principles, and that all human intimacy is rooted in the intimacy that we have with God. The God who became incarnate in Christ continues to live through the loving intimacy we have with one another.

Intimacy needs challenge parishes to develop viable youth ministry programs. Parish communities also need small Christian communities and support groups for young people. A catechist cannot teach effectively if the intimacy needs of the catechized are overlooked. It's as if the teacher was trying to fill up an empty container that leaked.

In a broad sense, "community" includes family and all human associations that have the "ultimate" as an important component of the relationships between members. Through the intimacy experienced in the Christian community, and with family and friends, incarnational catechesis becomes most effective. Such intimacy manifests the intimacy of the Risen Christ with His Father and with the Holy Spirit.

Family can be the ideal paradigm for other communities that strive to reflect the presence of the living Lord. The *Catechism of the Catholic Church* describes the family as a "privileged community called to achieve a 'sharing of thought and common deliberation by the spouses as well as their eager cooperation as parents in the children's upbringing'" (2206).

Changing family patterns present challenges. Working parents, business trips, children's activities, shopping after work, eating at fast-food restaurants are a few of the challenges. In single-parent and in blended families, many family members sometimes find it difficult to have enough quality time together. Not finding their needs met at home, people often look elsewhere for community. Many fulfill this need in legitimate ways — in small church gatherings, youth groups, and in other communities. Others find their outlets in drugs, unhealthy group associations, questionable friends, or illicit affairs.

Besides providing opportunities for community and for experiencing the presence of the risen Lord, catechists can encourage those catechized to find community in their neighborhoods, family gatherings, work situations, study or support groups, sports activities, assemblies, civic meetings, and retirement homes. Catechists can remind the catechized to look for God in their everyday lives, and in service to their brothers and sisters.

The catechized, even children and youths, are unfulfilled by functionally living alone. They search for ultimate meaning in the quest for love, peace, and quiet time. The catechized need to experience a welcoming spiritual atmosphere, not an efficiently run program.

The need for true and deeper fulfillment requires parish catechists to reexamine the way that Jesus treated people. He took time with them. He was sensitive to their needs. He taught them their personal worth before God. People seek the same response from our parishes.

During uncertain times, certitude and roots help people in their search for intimacy, meaning, and fulfillment. How can catechists assist the catechized in their search for certitude and roots? They can provide a climate where children and youths call upon God to give them deeper support than humans can give. This comes down to a matter of faith — the faith that a catechist evokes in the catechized. The risen Lord, alone, and His teaching provide the certitude that people need today.

Lack of respect for credible civic and Church authorities is a modern tragedy. Some leaders betrayed the public's trust through scandals, questionable politics, and the inability to cope with real issues. Reactions to recent scandals in the secular and religious arena have affected the reputation of authority figures in general. This changing attitude toward Church authority has profound ramifications for catechesis. Scandals involving bishops and priests, have eroded public confidence in Church authority. This is especially true when people sense a coverup, lack of honesty, or failure to support victims. This climate makes it difficult for Church authorities to lead, and for catechists to uphold the Church's teachings on morality, fidelity in marriage, and a host of other issues. When this happens, people do not find there the presence of the Incarnate Lord.

The feeling of disconnection is a growing phenomenon in the United States. People are disconnected from decision-makers in our country, from leaders of our Church, and from family members. With the mobility of our citizens on the rise, the family disconnect provides special challenges. Catechists can help the catechized see that they need never be disconnected from the living presence of Jesus who is incarnated in the Catholic community.

In addition to the issues mentioned above, catechists need to be particularly mindful of growing generational, ethnic, and family diversity. Other cultural realities that impact catechesis are the lack of denominational affiliation, a weakening belief in life's spiritual dimension, declining socialization at home, and declining participation at Sunday worship. All of these profoundly influence catechesis today. But in every instance, focusing on Jesus in our midst is an effective way to help the catechized recognize the Lord's presence living in their lives and actions.

Section 3:
BISHOPS' DIRECTIONS

In light of post-Vatican II catechesis and the U.S. bishops' Sub-committee on the Catechism, it is clear that the future direction of incarnational catechesis will be strongly focused on basic teachings of the Church. The protocols established by this subcommittee must be met by textbook publishers to satisfy the need for authenticity and completeness. In light of the protocols, textbooks must include all key components of Catholic belief and practice to satisfy the criteria for "conformity" to the language of the *Catechism of the Catholic Church*. Conformity norms explicitly state that a common language of faith should be developed in the Catholic Church. The hope is to establish a classical language for catechesis, and a common language of faith, analogous to the classical terminology of the *Baltimore Catechism* that was standard before Vatican II.

In so doing, it is hoped that future Catholics will be able to speak a common language of faith, as did Catholics before Vatican II — that is, transubstantiation, sanctifying grace, Extreme Unction. The subcommittee also requires that all religion textbooks include eight dimensions of authenticity, including, among other things, ecclesial balance and a Trinitarian focus, as well as five norms for completeness. This new orientation does not imply that catechesis should go back to earlier standards and style. It does mean taking the best of what once was and incorporating it into a new approach. This new approach is focused on the basic teachings and is rooted in incarnational catechesis.

The subcommittee's guidelines for the implementation of the *Catechism of the Catholic Church* do not insist that a particular belief be taught in a particular way. Rather, the guidelines are a clear and specific guide for catechetical content, as textbook publishers develop religion books, and as catechetical leaders design doctrinally balanced catechetical programs.

While incarnational catechesis provides a solid foundation to revitalize catechesis, it alone will not cure the Church's ills. A catechist's effectiveness is greatly influenced by the overall parish spirit and by the family situations of the catechized. A catechist alone cannot change a parish's lack of hospitality. Catechists can't compensate for the lack of faith in the homes of children who come for instruction.

Catechists have limited control over catechetical sessions. They can do their best to present God's Word in a clear, concise way and to encourage the catechized to respond. But, the rest is up to God, the parents, and the broader Church. As indicated before, the challenge today is to acknowledge the real Catholic climate of parishes and families, and to catechize within it.

CHAPTER 7

COMMON SENSE CATECHESIS (SYSTEMATIC – PERSONALISTIC)

"It's not proselytism that makes the Church grow. It's testimony."

(Pope Francis, *Address to International Catechetical Congress*, September 27, 2013)

At one time, many staff members of diocesan religious education offices were personally engaged in catechetical formation. They went into parishes and other venues to offer courses on basic teachings and catechetical approaches. In 1976, when I directed the religious education office in Cincinnati, we had about twenty-seven staff members. With this staff, the office offered many courses and entered into cooperative ventures with professional directors of religious education and college professors. Something similar happened in other dioceses. In later years, with diminishing financial resources, dioceses cut the size of their offices.

The glory days of diocesan religious education are over. Today, many dioceses often employ only a few staff people.

Some offices have closed, drastically changed, or been assimilated into other offices. Many today are called the Office of Evangelization and Catechesis. Such changes have deep-seated ramifications for parish catechesis. Also, due to fewer financial resources, a similar downsized outreach exists in many parishes. Volunteer parish catechists are less likely to be trained with solid, comprehensive knowledge of basic Church teaching.

While the bishops' Subcommittee on the Catechism stresses the message and language of faith, a big question remains. How will ordinary catechists, with limited contact with professional religious educators, be able to share the faith fully? The answer is that catechists need to be well versed in basic information, not sophisticated theories about how and what to teach.

With this in mind, the way of catechizing today must be clear, simple, and understandable to the volunteer catechist.

To effectively renew catechesis in the United States, two major factors that changed catechesis after Vatican II must be considered. The first is the movement to a more open society. This point is critical for it brings new challenges from the secular world. Clearly, we must have a different way to present the Christian message. In the 1970s and 1980s, different approaches addressed this goal. In the 1990s, the Church refocused catechesis in light of the *Catechism of the Catholic Church* and the *General Directory for Catechesis*.

The second factor is the significance of secular influences on Catholics, and the importance of connecting catechesis with the world that the catechized deal with every day.

This final chapter offers a new approach to catechesis in four sections. Section 1 describes the Common Sense (Systematic – Personalistic) Approach. Section 2 gives examples of how this approach works by considering preparation and presentation. Section 3 looks at digital technology and catechesis, and Section 4 offers further reflections.

Section 1:
THE COMMON SENSE (SYSTEMATIC – PERSONALISTIC) APPROACH TO CATECHESIS

During *Baltimore Catechism* times, the Catholic climate was the fundamental dynamic that kept Catholics in close association with the Church and with other Catholics. When this shifted, something more was required. This shift put greater stress on families and the parish community to provide the stability that the Catholic climate once offered.

A real challenge occurs when neither the Catholic climate nor the parish community is strong. When this happens, more responsibility is put on parents and catechists to help the catechized. This is a real challenge if parents aren't interested, and if catechists have limited time to prepare. With this in mind, today's parishes need to be realistic about what they ask of catechists. They must help them maximize their efforts in the time they have.

The Common Sense (Systematic – Personalistic) Approach to catechesis begins with the presupposition that most catechists are ordinary people — well-intentioned, willing to study and learn, but without much formal background in theology or catechesis. This does not imply that they are not good catechists. Just the opposite is often true. Many know what they are teaching and do a good job teaching it. But they need direction. Some volunteer parish catechists are also elementary school teachers or well-prepared high school religion teachers. They already know successful ways of teaching and apply them to catechetical instruction. But most catechists, even some who teach religion in Catholic elementary schools, have a minimal amount of catechetical training. The common sense approach enhances what they are already doing, rather than suggesting new ways that are unrealizable for them.

It's important to encourage catechists to prepare as well as possible. They are encouraged to take courses for catechists sponsored by the diocese or another educational institution or program. Most catechists are volunteers and work without pay. They do their best in the time they have. Many do not have the time, money, or energy to take classes or spend prolonged time in preparing to be catechists. Often, their preparation is limited to reading the catechetical text ahead of time, getting ideas on the Internet, gathering audiovisuals, preparing prayers, and receiving suggestions from other catechists.

Today, catechesis, like the Church generally, is bombarded by pressures and tensions brought on by the secular values that engulf Catholics. These include, among others, the desire for bigger and better homes and cars, as well as questionable advertizing, the use of pornography, the threat of terrorism, and sexually alluring clothing. How do catechists deal with such challenges when the catechetical message is contrary to what children, youths, and adults face every day?

Rather than propose an idealized way of doing catechesis, common sense catechesis looks at the actual situation of the catechist. Why devise a theoretical way to catechize if it is unrealistic? Saying this does not talk down to volunteer catechists. It accepts their situations as they actually exist, and suggests a realistic way of catechizing that can be understood and applied by catechists themselves.

Catechists live in the secular world and recognize its good and negative values. A major task for catechists is to sift the culture for positive values, and then to reinforce them for the catechized. Catechists must also challenge negative values and show how Jesus' message is the antidote for secular values run wild.

What then can be said about the common sense approach to catechesis?

This approach presumes that Christ is at the center of all catechetical activity. Consequently, all catechetical sessions focus in some way on Scripture and how the Old and New Testaments invite us to learn about Jesus and His message. In listening to the biblical word and how the Catholic Church interprets it, common sense catechesis urges the catechized to discover the Lord and the implications of His teaching in their lives. This discovery process helps them know who they are as Catholics and enhances their Catholic identity. Finally, common sense catechesis helps the catechized reach out to others and share Jesus' message of love through their lives, sacrifice, and work.

Common sense catechesis requires that we keep in mind the conclusions found in incarnational catechesis as they were presented in Chapter 6. Those conclusions are that catechesis should:

- Focus on the being or nature of Jesus.

- See the crucifixion as the culmination of divine love.

- Connect Jesus' radical love on the cross with His ongoing presence in the Eucharist.

- Recognize that all faithful Christians live as other Christs in union with each other as the Body of Christ, the Church.

- Stress Jesus' call to serve the poor as a central aspect of being His disciple.

- Challenge catechists to teach the catechetical message in understandable language, and incorporate it into the appropriate cultural context.

- Root incarnational theology in the Trinity.

The Risen Christ ministers through the catechetical community. The catechized are made in the divine image. They are to center their lives and catechetical learning on Christ. The catechist is privileged to share God's Word. What is taught presumes that the living Word of God touches the hearts of the catechized in whatever cultural context they live, for God is present in this ministry. The risen Lord is incarnated in every catechetical community that meets in the name of Jesus to learn the Good News.

For all of this to happen, effective catechesis requires two things of the catechist. First of all, the catechist must know the basic teachings to be taught. Second, he or she must devise ways to present these teachings clearly and effectively to the catechized. Catechesis is not complex, unless we make it so. If we begin with these two common sense perspectives, everything else fits into place. Catechesis comes alive. Without them, catechesis is often ineffective.

This approach is in keeping with what the *General Directory for Catechesis* proposes. Christian hope roots this common sense approach. It gives energy to catechetical sessions and transforms sessions which can otherwise be boring, and fills them with life.

Before reflecting on the best ways to teach, we must consider how Jesus catechized. After He called His disciples, He did not send them off for a two-year program in a Hebrew school for Pharisees. No, they stayed with Him and learned from His example. Even on the Road to Emmaus, He catechized two disciples and showed them how the ancient prophesies were fulfilled in Him. Later, after Pentecost, He did not wait until His followers knew all the nuances of the Old Testament before He sent them to proclaim His message to all nations.

The technical name given to common sense catechesis is Systematic – Personalistic Catechesis. The words themselves reflect the current direction taken by the bishops' Subcommittee on the Catechism.

Systematic

The first term, "*systematic*," refers to teaching basic Church teachings and following a regular progression of instruction, usually prepared by professionals, including the bishops' Subcommittee on the Catechism. This committee developed protocols for textbooks that the authors and publishers follow. These protocols are well thought out and refined for use in catechetical texts. It is recommended that catechetical leaders or catechists study various texts and choose one that fits their needs.

Where diocesan or other graded courses of study exist, catechists should follow them and apply them. They contain valuable information. They save catechists a great deal of time that they would have spent if they had to develop the sequence of teaching on their own. With textbooks and other catechetical materials as guides, catechists can develop lesson plans and choose appropriate supplementary materials.

The beginning point of a catechist's preparation is not human experience but the message to be taught. That message is centered in Christ. It's the basic teaching that's important. The catechist begins by studying Scripture and other materials to be taught, and by trying to thoroughly understand them. After that, the catechist devises ways to help the catechized understand and apply these lessons to their lives. How this is done will vary from catechist to catechist, situation to situation. There is no one magical way to catechize. The chief goal of catechetical sessions is to teach the basic teachings of the Church and show how they apply to life.

Personalistic

The second term, "personalistic," refers to teaching basic Catholic belief in such a way that it is understood and can be applied by the catechized. This means teaching the Word of God in such a way that the Gospel will have a "real impact on God's faithful people and the concrete needs of the present time" (*Evangelii Gaudium*, Pope Francis, No. 95). Here, in particular, the catechetical message becomes incarnational. The message must be personalized and applied to life. This means helping students understand its implications for their own lives, and helping them to see how Jesus' teachings give the catechized a firm rudder to steer through the engulfing waves of secularism. This requires:

1) The catechist must be thoroughly acquainted with and understand what is to be taught, especially within a biblical and Church context. It may take considerable preparation on the part of the catechist to understand the background materials and learn them.

2) The catechist must know the challenges facing the catechized, and devise ways to get the basic teaching or message across to the student. In other words, the materials taught must be age and context appropriate. The catechetical presentation must bring in the experience and life situation of the catechized. But the primary purpose of catechesis is to teach the basics of the faith, not to share experience for experience sake. Experience is shared to the extent that it enhances the lesson to be learned and incarnates the Word of God in the lives of the catechized. In this regard, storytelling is a valuable way to connect what is taught to the life and interests of the catechized.

Helping the catechized understand the message within the context of life is the task of every good catechist. This includes using the terminology of faith taken from the *Catechism of the Catholic Church,* explaining it, and putting it into language that today's children, teenagers, and adults can understand. For instance, it's not sufficient for a catechist to teach children that Jesus is "consubstantial" with the Father. The catechist must first understand what this term means. He or she must know that both Jesus and the Father have the same divine substance, or nature, analogous to how the teacher and students have the same human substance, or nature. The Father, the Son, and the Holy Spirit have the same divine nature, and are one God. In the one God, there are three divine persons in one divine nature. In other words, there is one God in three persons. Even though this is a mystery, the teacher can devise ways to help students understand what it means. Good lessons can get this across to the catechized in language that they understand. Students must also learn how important it is to keep God alive and active in their lives.

Religious women who taught the *Baltimore Catechism* when we were children followed a similar approach. They first studied and learned the lessons ahead of time. They got advice from books and other teachers, and then taught it to us. They made sure that we understood what it meant as it referred to our lives. They often learned how to do this from older, more experienced sisters or at Saturday seminars in their convents. Today, catechists can also learn how to do it from more experienced teachers. They can attend catechetical sessions sponsored by parishes or the diocese. If catechists are strapped for time, they may have to learn it on their own through reading, through other types of preparation, and perhaps through online resources.

Many dioceses offer a regular sequence of courses required to get certification as a catechist or catechetical leader. These teach excellent methods for making catechetical sessions more vibrant. They need to be supplemented by reading and more in-depth study, especially as a catechist continues to teach over a period of time. Here is where online Catholic information and courses can help catechists to be more effective.

To address the needs of busy catechetical leaders, parish ministers, and catechists, online courses, sponsored by Catholic academic institutions and other agencies, can be valuable.

It's now possible to take entire courses — for example, a course on sacraments — for credit or enrichment. These courses have been well put together and taught by skilled teachers and on-line communicators. These courses incorporate an ongoing interaction with instructors and other students.

One such program is offered by the University of Dayton. It is called VLCFF (Virtual Learning Community Faith Formation). The goal of this virtual learning community is "to support the church's professional ministry of religious education and faith formation in cyberspace." Seven five-week cycles of courses are offered each year. Participants from all over the world take part in each session. These courses provide a good source for adult faith formation, catechist certification, and training for catechetical leaders and catechists. Efforts such as these fit in well with our fast-paced cyberworld and reflect a realistic approach to the needs of modern catechesis.

Such virtual learning communities play an important role in common sense catechesis.

Section 2:
COMMON SENSE CATECHESIS
IN ACTION

This section is divided into two main parts: preparing catechists and parents, and conducting the catechetical session. Both are necessary for vibrant and effective catechesis.

Preparing Parents and Catechists

Catechetical preparation takes different forms among parents and catechists. Parents play a central role in the faith formation of their children. So, it's good to begin with their preparation. Both are needed in a successful catechetical venture.

Parental Preparation

Recently, my sister and I attended a Sunday liturgy in a Catholic parish while on vacation. We got to the church early, and sat near the back of church. Before Mass began, I observed that about 75 percent of the attendees were from the *Baltimore Catechism* era. They were friendly to each other, and it was apparent that this parish was active and enthusiastic. We could soon see that around 20 percent of the congregation were younger parishioners and about 5 percent were children or teenagers.

I reflected on this congregation in light of their probable catechetical formation. The older group fell into the category of people growing up in the pre-Vatican II Catholic climate. They were devout and prayerful and had just finished saying the Rosary as we entered the church. The Rosary before Mass was followed by other prayers.

I imagined that these folks learned their prayers and basic Catholic instruction from the *Baltimore Catechism*. They probably learned about their faith early in life and cherished that faith to this day. I suspect that their parents had taught them Catholic prayers and had listened to their catechism lessons when they went to school. Only later, did they learn the full meaning of the prayers and instructions they were taught at an early age.

Regarding the younger group of parents, the picture was not as clear. No doubt, many of the 20 percent were influenced by a strong Catholic home. The parents had probably taken these people to church when they were children. It's likely that they were taught to pray some prayers at home. This group, along with the older group, probably included those who went to Bible study classes. They may have engaged in other adult faith formation programs just to learn more about their faith.

Finally, I thought about the few children and teenagers present in this church with their parents. I wondered what would happen to them. How many of this 5 percent would remain Catholic in the future?

As I thought of them, I realized that the key questions were: "What can parents and parishes offer this young generation in the way of prayer and instruction? How can we help them to face the secular world and maintain a stable foundation in the faith?" As I sat in church before Mass, I became more convinced of the value of common sense catechesis. Solid catechetical instruction must be based on teaching children and teenagers a core group of prayers and basic Church teachings, especially teachings about Christ's presence in the Eucharist. Learning these is absolutely necessary and roots a person's appreciation of the Catholic faith.

In considering the key elements of the common sense approach, it is vital to remember that catechetical sessions are profoundly affected by how parents catechize their children. Parishes must concentrate on helping families accept their catechetical responsibilities. The parish supports, but doesn't replace, parents in the catechetical endeavor. There is no one way to do this. Catechesis in the home depends on parental and family configurations. It also depends on whether parents catechize their children because they know this is a vital part of their own Christian vocation.

As I sat in this church with my sister, I wondered how many parents sitting there taught their children prayers from the time they were very young. The prayers could have been — simple, spontaneous prayers, like "God, help my family," or "Jesus, I love you." As their children matured, how many adults in this church had taught their sons and daughters the Our Father and the Hail Mary? When they started school, how many children were encouraged to learn the Act of Contrition, or how to say the Rosary?

I remembered my parents teaching me these prayers. As a child, I presumed that all parents did that. But I learned later that this was not the case. In retrospect, the prayers my parents taught me, even if I do not remember how they did it, set the foundation for my faith. It helped me turn to God when I was in need.

Parents play a vital role in catechizing their families. They set the tone, and, as far as possible, catechists must connect with them. Parents are the key to determining the success of catechetical ministry.

Catechesis must be rooted in a person's prayer life. So, catechetical and adult faith formation for parents themselves must be taken very seriously. Many parents know very little about the faith. This lack of knowledge sometimes makes them reluctant to discuss faith issues with their children. Hence, parishes need to devise ways to help parents be comfortable with what they believe so that they can teach their children. When parents teach their children to pray they do more than help them say the words. They give children a way to deal with various life events. Parental faith tells children in spoken and unspoken words that there is a world beyond the one they perceive with their eyes, ears, and senses.

Children and youths today need a foundation in prayer. Prayer is a starting point for a better appreciation of a renewed

Catholic climate. It is essential for faithfulness to God and active Church involvement. Reading Part Four of the *Catechism of the Catholic Church* provides an excellent basis for a better understanding of prayer, and its role in the Christian life.

In addition to teaching me how to pray, I remember the small religion books that my parents bought me. These little books taught me simple faith statements, like "God exists," "God is all good," "Jesus loves me so much that He died for me." I also read and learned that I am made in God's image and that the Holy Spirit helps me when I am in need. Finally, I learned that while this life is important, I was made for a fuller life. Someday I will be with God in heaven.

When I made my first Communion, I received a wonderful little first Communion prayer book from my grandmother. I would bring it to church every Sunday, and I still have and cherish it today. When I prayed from it before I went to Communion, I felt important. Along with this prayer book, my parents gave me a beautiful rosary. Such symbols of faith catechized me more than the lessons that I learned from the catechism.

As I grew into adolescence, Dad and Mom gave me other religious books for Christmas and for my birthday. I sometimes quote from one of them when speaking to catechists. It is called *The Man Who Dared a King*. It was about the life and death of Saint John Fisher, who was executed for his faith during the reign of King Henry VIII of England. In the book, John Fisher talked about his choice of being a priest. I wonder if his words put the seeds of a vocation into my mind at an early age.

From my childhood experiences I realized that we learn all through our lives. Rarely do we stop and ask, "How did I learn this or that?" We have a built-in capacity to learn, and this is the ordinary way we assimilate life events. We can use this built-in capacity to learn for catechesis. When we reflect on how we learn other things, we see that its no different than learning about our faith through catechesis.

Catechist Preparation

In his homily at the Mass for the Day of Catechists for the Year of Faith, celebrated in St. Peter's Square, September 29, 2013, Pope Francis asked: "Who are catechists? They are people who keep the memory of God alive; they keep it alive in themselves and they are able to revive it in others."

The pope continued:

> Faith contains our own memory of God's history with us, the memory of our encountering God who always takes the first step, who creates, saves and transforms us…. A catechist is a Christian who puts this remembrance at the service of proclamation. The catechist, then, is a Christian who is mindful of God, who is guided by the memory of God in his or her entire life and who is able to awaken that memory in the hearts of others.

Effective catechesis of children, youths, and adults requires that catechists are well-prepared people of faith. The best example of how to catechize comes from Jesus and His way of teaching people. He never turned them off. He took them where they were, and proceeded from there. He chose simple men and women — saints and sinners — and called them to serve as His first catechists. They were effective because they had faith, knew Jesus, learned from Him, and applied His teachings to life. In a similar way faith, life experiences, and serious preparation help good catechists today.

Catechesis includes more than what is taught – the content. Nonetheless, the "what" or basic teaching is vital. It includes information and transformation. The way catechists convey the message of faith to others depends on their talents, orientation, personality, and knowledge of Scripture and Church teaching. The Holy Spirit invites catechists to share their faith and to do their best to develop fruitful ways to bring the message of faith to the catechized.

Following Vatican II, some catechists forgot that learning the truths of the faith is a vital aspect of conversion. Reflecting on the fundamental tenets of faith as revealed in Scripture and sacred Tradition is an important aspect of coming closer to Jesus and growing in faith. Many people are drawn into the Catholic Church through her teachings and through study of the Church's history. This indicates that learning basic Church teachings is in itself a step to conversion. Studying Scripture and basic Church teachings, however, is not the end of catechesis.

Other aspects of catechesis include prayer, knowledge of social justice teaching, celebrating the Eucharist, and understanding the sacraments. All of these work in conjunction with learning basic Church beliefs and are directed to conversion.

A catechist's personal and spiritual preparation is ongoing. Living a good life is the best remote preparation for effective catechists. Sooner or later, a catechist's personal values, like authenticity and honesty, come across in catechetical sessions. Striving to live as a good Catholic does not mean that a catechist has to be perfect. At the same time, since catechists share Jesus' Word, this requires seriousness on their spiritual journey. Some catechists are further along than others on their spiritual journey. As long as they strive to follow the Lord, even catechists who sometimes fail can be good catechists.

Personal and spiritual growth go hand in hand. Catechists prepare every day to share God's Word through prayer and through the quality of their lives. They live in an upright, not scandalous, way so that those catechized can see the kind of Christian values that set the stage for following the Lord.

Catechists prepare all through life. But when a person is called to be a catechist, this requires special, additional preparation. Catechists are encouraged to take special catechetical classes, or attend workshops sponsored by the diocesan catechetical office. These educational offerings might also be given by the parish catechetical director, or by a local college or university. Catechists should be certified, if possible.

Prayer roots effective catechesis. Hence, the catechist prays to the Holy Spirit for wisdom before preparing to teach a basic Church teaching like the Communion of Saints, the Trinity, Mass, or baptism. In prayer, the catechist discerns ways to make a basic teaching understandable.

Along with parents, catechists are responsible to teach the catechized to pray. The catechist's role supplements that of the parents. Unfortunately, many parents do not pray with their children. This places an added responsibility on the catechist who then needs to help parents learn how to pray with their children.

Catechists need to incorporate Scripture into catechetical lessons. Each session can begin with reading and reflection on Scripture that is appropriate to the materials taught during a particular session. Brief lessons about or references to Scripture can also be interspersed within the catechetical lesson. Catechists are to teach basic Church beliefs in a clear and concise way.

Because some children attend catechetical sessions sporadically, and some catechists are not well instructed, pastors need to supervise catechetical programs to see that children receive solid catechetical instruction. This is especially true when children are preparing to receive a sacrament. Catechists should see to it that children do not cut corners in their catechetical preparation. If children are not attending classes, catechists should encourage children's parents to teach them the materials missed when they were not in class.

It is recommended that a list of prayers, Scripture passages, and basic teachings be developed for sessions taught over a period of time. This list can be prepared by a diocesan office, textbook publisher, parish catechetical leader, pastor, or a catechist. This list can be part of a course of studies. What students learn in one catechetical class needs to be consistent with what they learn in other catechetical classes. In this way, as the child grows in the knowledge of the faith, he or she will learn all the basic prayers and Church teachings. These teachings can be reviewed every year so that the child and family can internalize and integrate them into their lives.

Preparing to catechize requires significant time and study on the part of the catechist. Imagine that a catechist is going to catechize eighth-graders on a more difficult subject, like the Communion of Saints. How does one begin and proceed?

Catechetical preparation for teaching eighth-graders this Church teaching requires more than a cursory look at a textbook before class. If the class is using a textbook approved by the bishops' catechism committee, it contains a section on the Communion of Saints. When going through the teacher's manual, the catechist will learn that this teaching has two meanings.

The first and most common meaning of the Communion of Saints refers to the union of the saints in heaven together with the members of the Church on earth and the souls in purgatory. Sometimes these three groups are called the "Church Triumphant" (saints in heaven), the "Church Militant" (Church on earth), and the "Church Suffering" (souls in purgatory). This most common use of the expression the Communion of Saints refers to the communion or unity of holy people. This is the only meaning that most people know. Catechists must understand this basic teaching so that they can teach it effectively. Catholics should understand that the Communion of Saints means that those in purgatory, on earth, and in heaven are bound in a special fellowship.

In the Eucharist, we enter into communion with Christ and with each other. This can be illustrated by giving the catechized examples of how fellowship between friends is solidified by caring for each other. It is also seen in families when family members help and sacrifice for each other. In addition, the catechist can prepare questions and exercises to help the catechized reflect on what this basic teaching means for them. What implications does the Communion of Saints have, as they pray and face good and hard times?

A second meaning of the Communion of Saints refers to a "communion in holy things." This meaning dates from the early Church and continued through later centuries. What are these "holy things"? Holy things refer primarily to the Eucharist. Those who share in the Eucharist become holy people by virtue of their sharing in it. Through the Eucharist, they are united as a body of believers.

The catechist should reflect beforehand on both meanings of the Communion of Saints, and devise ways to explain it. The catechist could explain that when we receive the Eucharist, we enter into communion with Christ and with each other. This gives the catechized a foundation for why they are to help one another and celebrate their accomplishments.

Furthermore, the catechist considers what this means for those present. He or she can develop questions and activities for use with the catechized. These can help to highlight the wonder of the Eucharist, and can help teach how the Eucharist helps us live holy and upright lives. This belief underscores the importance of going to Mass often and receiving the Eucharist. To better prepare for this or any other catechetical session, the catechist should study how catechetical books present this basic teaching, and what practical lessons can be drawn for the catechized.

After the catechist studies this basic belief carefully, he or she is ready to present it. When both meanings of the Communion of Saints are presented, the catechized can see that holy people share in holy things.

Conducting the Catechetical Session

Here, we consider the actual catechetical session, and how to approach it. The focus is on teaching the catechetical truths. This also requires arranging and preparing the setting where catechesis will take place.

The Environment

The place where catechesis happens is important. Environment affects the communication that takes place within it. If a room is clean and nicely arranged, it produces an immediate, positive effect on those entering. The unconscious reaction is, "Something important and good will happen here." That's why a catechist must prepare a welcoming, fresh environment for the catechized.

When entering a classroom, those who will be catechized should never see a dirty garbage can or an unkempt room that looks more like a storage space than a classroom. We never welcome people into our homes in this way. So why would we let anyone come into a catechetical session in this sort of setting?

I remember how nice, clean, and beautifully decorated the rooms were where we had religion classes when I was a child. The sisters made sure of it. The same must be true of the places where catechesis happens today. When I directed the Cincinnati religious office, one catechist told me that the only parish space she could call her own was an old broom closet. There she stored her catechetical materials. She didn't even have the regular use of the basement classroom where she catechized. What does this say about this parish's priority given to catechesis?

Catechists and the catechized have a right to a welcoming environment. Catechists can partner with teachers in the Catholic school if they use the same rooms. This environment can be welcoming to both religious education and Catholic school students.

The catechist is encouraged to put a crucifix in the room if there isn't one. Catechists should also decorate the room with appropriate Catholic symbols, religious pictures, and statues. It's easy to forget, in this fact-oriented world, that symbols are important ways to communicate. Learning goes far beyond the rational facts that our society depends on. Religious facts are necessary in catechesis, but they must be presented as part of a broader, more holistic approach to faith.

Conducting the Session

The catechist should arrive for the catechetical session in plenty of time. He or she must check over the physical environment, making sure that the lights work and that the visual aids, computers, interactive technology, and other equipment are in place and ready for use. If not, the catechist should know where to get needed materials and assistance. When the catechized begin arriving, the catechist welcomes them and any parents or others who come to the room to drop off the children.

No two catechists catechize in exactly the same way. But regardless of the approach used, it is essential to convey the basic teachings of the faith. Catechists must help the catechized understand, internalize, and apply these teachings to life. Some catechists may initially focus on the basic teachings. Later they show the catechized how they are applied to life. Other catechists may tell a personal story first. They consider the experience of those being catechized, and then apply the basic teaching to what has been discussed.

Regardless of the catechist's approach, when the session is ready to begin, the teacher should quiet down the class. This is the time for everyone to put themselves in God's presence. Then, an appropriate prayer or biblical text begins the session. The catechist and the catechized reflect on the Scripture text together. The catechized are reminded that the Word of God is vibrant and alive and speaks to us. God is present in the Word. Catechists reiterate that the living, breathing Word of God speaks to all present in their lives. Openness to the Word sets the climate for the catechetical session that follows. Before the class begins, the catechist has selected this biblical text or a prayer that leads naturally into the lesson.

If the catechist has not done so at the very beginning of the session, he or she can now make announcements. Then students are told what will be happening during the class. A brief review of what took place the in previous class follows. This is intended for those who missed the previous session, and as a summary for those who attended. If students were assigned reading material beforehand or given other assignments, the catechist asks them about their work and answers the questions they have.

There is an approach that catechists should avoid. It is not helpful to spend the entire class time lecturing to eighth-graders or any other age group. This bores and distracts them, often leading to class disturbances.

At the proper time, the catechist begins to teach the new lesson, for instance, a lesson on the Communion of Saints. The catechist presents the basic beliefs that the catechist prepared at home. The session includes time for the presentation of materials, discussions, questions, previously assigned student activities, including those of a digital nature, and those taken from the textbook or other sources.

Appropriate materials about the Communion of Saints, found in student books, on the Internet, or through social media can be used to illustrate and discuss both meanings of this term. (iPods or iPads can be used). The entire catechetical session must be informative and interesting. It must take into account the students' needs, experiences, and backgrounds. The catechist should engage students in discussion, raising questions, and asking for student reactions. When possible, personal stories or appropriate stories of the lives of the saints can be shared.

In presenting the Communion of Saints, or any other topic, the catechist must be sensitive to students' family situations and discretely handle situations like parental divorce/remarriage or students who rarely attend Mass. The materials taught have to be accurate and consistent with what is contained in the *Catechism of the Catholic Church*. At the same time, the lessons should take into account the backgrounds of the catechized, and the challenges of contemporary culture. When fitting, the catechist discusses delicate matters privately with certain students.

Catechists should deal with questions that children, youths, and adults ask. However, they must be careful not to raise sensitive issues that are beyond the age and intellectual comprehension of the catechized. In other words, what catechists teach must be age appropriate. This does not mean that catechists limit themselves only to a student's immediate concerns. There's no need to avoid addressing issues and challenges that students will encounter in the future. It means that catechists should teach aspects of the faith that will have future significance to the catechized in an understandable and meaningful way.

Every catechetical session contains a personal dimension. This could be no more than showing concern for those present. This is important when dealing with certain issues. You may have a child in class whose parents are seriously ill. There may be parents who are grieving over the death of a child or another family member. When catechists show concern, the catechized are more likely to understand God's love, and what the catechist teaches. Finally, in every catechetical session, the catechist is encouraged to tell stories and share personal experiences. These keep student attention and foster learning and the conversion process.

When possible, the catechist links the materials taught with the liturgy, especially the Eucharist. He or she also presents the Church's social teaching, pointing out that what is taught inevitably leads us to worship and praise God as well as service to our brothers and sisters.

Near the end of the class, the catechist reviews what was taught with the catechized. Information pertaining to class teachings is sent home to the parents. Parents can continue the conversation with their children in the home. Finally, after giving assignments for the next class, the catechist says a prayer and dismisses the students. After class, the catechist may talk to students or parents who wish to discuss a child's progress. They might also find themselves helping students who missed class or didn't understand what was taught.

Sacramental preparation is an important aspect of the catechetical ministry. Care must be taken to make it a wonderful opportunity for children and parents to hear God's Word and celebrate it in the sacraments they are about to receive.

In adult faith formation, as illustrated in the Rite of Christian Initiation of Adults, biblical stories, personal stories, and the experiences of those present are significant. The catechist helps the catechized recognize how God is present in their stories. They also show how the Word of God and basic Catholic teachings help adults, youths, and children recognize Jesus' presence and understand His message. Other ways of catechizing can also include the common sense approach described in this section. This approach can be applied to a family-centered catechesis or many other ways of catechizing.

Section 3:
DIGITAL TECHNOLOGY AND CATECHESIS

Common sense catechesis must be integrated into the lives of the catechized. In the present era, this means that it must include a component of digital technology. While this is necessary, catechists are to avoid certain pitfalls described here. At the same time, making use of digital technology is certainly a "must" for catechists.

A Must for Tomorrow

The Introduction to this book states:

> Digital technology is changing society. It's shifting how we think and act. In the midst of this revolution, catechesis must change. If not, the Word of God will go unheard by countless people around the world.
>
> As we look to the future and ask what these changes will entail, we also remember the past. From history, we learn important lessons, as new methods and ways of catechizing emerge. Consequently, this book begins with a challenge. Can we get insights into the new catechetical directions from what has happened after Vatican II? (p. 20)

Today's catechesis must take two things into account. The first is the requirements to focus on basic Church teaching while employing the language of the *Catechism of the Catholic Church*. The second issue is to increase the use of various kinds of digital technology to convey the content of the Catholic faith in light of today's culture.

After Vatican II, a great deal of energy was expended on the "how" of catechesis — what teaching methods should be used. The U.S. bishops published guidelines for basic catechetical instruction called *Basic Teachings for Catholic Religious Education.* These received limited emphasis in catechetical circles. Instead, many catechists seemed more interested in new ways to teach, having realized that the *Baltimore Catechism* approach was to be changed.

Today, catechists must hear and follow the catechetical directives that come from the bishops of the Unites States. Basic Catholic teaching must be conveyed in a clear and accurate way. Catechists should not sacrifice basic teaching when focusing on new methods of catechizing through digital technology.

This does not mean that catechists are to avoid the new digital technology. Just the opposite is true. When using it, however, catechists must provide complete and exact catechesis. Both solid catechetical content and new digital means of conveying it must work side by side. If we use certain forms of online catechesis, for example, we must see the big picture when concentrating on a certain Church teaching. The same is true for catechists developing an interactive program that concentrates on only one aspect of Catholicism.

Contrasting today's catechetical situation with what existed in the 1970s has much merit. After Vatican II, many changes occurred that required new directions. The focus on experience and methodology attempted to come to grips with the new situation. Unfortunately, many catechists missed the critical piece. They didn't stress basic Church teaching while moving to new methods. If catechists are not careful, a similar thing can occur today as they move into a new digital era. When learning how to effectively teach by using digital technology, catechists must make sure that all the basic teachings of the Church are conveyed. We can't present just the easiest or most popular ones, like social justice issues, new prayer forms, and suchlike. For example, catechists can and should give solid reasons why premarital sex is wrong, and why the Church opposes abortion, same-sex marriage, and artificial birth control.

It's not a question of whether or not we should use the new digital technology. It's here, and we must employ it catechetically to effectively communicate the Word of God. It is one of the most important new "means" to teach the basic doctrine of the Church. It's a question of "how" we can best use it, not "if" we will use it.

In saying this, however, we remember that the Catholic faith is a community-based one. No catechesis based on technology alone, used in isolation or apart from a believing community, can be truly Catholic. A built-in communal dynamic in the new digital technology moves people to interface on podcasts, use social media, Skype, and other methods that bring them together. The cybercommunity that is formed, however, is not sufficient in itself.

A central goal of catechesis is to bring people together face-to-face to share Catholic beliefs, celebrate the sacraments, pray, and serve one another. Digital catechesis can help teach abstract faith beliefs presented in the *Catechism of the Catholic Church*. However, this teaching must be done in interpersonal ways so that those catechized can worship, support one another, and grow in a flesh-and-blood community.

New Technology and Catechesis

In an article published in the January 2013 issue of *Catechetical Leader* magazine, Sr. Angela Ann Zukowski wrote about the new technology in catechesis. She said, "New learning environments, supported by the Internet, virtual opportunities and new methodologies are transforming students' ways of thinking, learning, and being." In the context of this reality, "Computer and mobile technology resources [such] as iPods, iPhones, iPads, e-books, and vast, burgeoning assortments of apps are being woven into the general curriculum" ("We Never Did It That Way," p. 12).

These are the tools of the future for new catechetical methodologies. We must use them, but not as ends in themselves. They must be a means to convey God's Word in a community of faith. God's Word needs to be incorporated into any learning environment a catechist faces — from early childhood to adult faith formation.

Since younger Catholics often process information differently than older Catholics, what we teach them must be consistent with how they learn. Youths use a different language and mode of communication. We must utilize the ways they learn to teach them basic Catholic beliefs. We must engage them in interactive lessons on the topics being taught, like the beatitudes, Communion of Saints, Eucharist and all the major beliefs of the Church. We must then bring them together interpersonally to pray, learn, and serve. Through digital technology, those catechized can better appreciate that they are part of a universal Catholic community. They can see in a new way how they are members of the Mystical Body of Christ.

The digital revolution affords ample opportunities for catechesis. The challenge is to acknowledge this and to devise ways to use technology to enhance the faith of Christians of every age and place. In particular, digital catechesis offers many possibilities for adult faith formation and for the catechesis of children and youth. Because we live in a new age, catechesis cannot use only one technique or approach. In the era of digital technology, catechesis must be unified, multifaceted, and flexible.

Common sense catechesis takes its origin from where the catechists are in their lives and helps them learn and integrate basic Church teachings that they convey to the catechized. Today, this generally requires a rudimentary use of the new digital technology. For this reason, those directing parish catechetical programs need to help catechists learn what is required and make sure that all the fundamentals of the faith are included.

As far as children and young people are concerned, most are already engaged with the new digital technology. They use it in school and have grown up with it. Consequently, a catechist must inform them of solid catechetical materials that are available online and help them to understand and apply them to their lives. To do this, interactive digital technology between the students in and outside of a catechetical setting is valuable.

The use of the media grows in catechesis, since the Internet and social networking are important ways that young people communicate. Those sensitive to the way children and teenagers relate to one another indicate that if future catechetical lessons are not on iPads and other modes of communication, catechists may not be very successful in teaching students. Catechetical leaders and producers of catechetical materials need to get in line with the way this generation shares information. This can be done without neglecting the significance of relationships as a key to successful evangelization.

Catechists need to make sure that when they use new forms of media these connect the catechized with a living community of believers in the parish or school. This is especially true in multiethnic contexts. The influx of Hispanics, Asians, and other ethnic groups challenges parishes to incorporate the richness of these traditions into catechetical sessions. It also challenges catechists to be sensitive to the ways that these groups learn and celebrate the Catholic faith.

The ultimate success of future catechesis will require that parents assume a greater responsibility for preparing their children in the faith. They need to address their spiritual hungers as they mature.

Section 4:
LOOKING BACKWARD AND FORWARD

When considering the challenges to catechesis in the twenty-first century, it is worth remembering that before Vatican II the religious formation of children did not occur only through learning the *Baltimore Catechism*. Rather, children were formed through the whole Catholic climate. It's a mistake to conclude that inadequate catechesis of the past thirty-five years is the main reason why many of today's Catholics do not go to church.

Catechesis never carried the primary burden for the faith formation of Catholics. Formation occurs primarily in the family, and then in the whole Catholic community. When the Catholic climate was firm and strong, religious formation naturally happened and the *Baltimore Catechism* easily fit into this picture. Now this climate had changed. In fact, it scarcely exists in some places.

Catechesis has a formative aspect. Its aim is to convey basic truths of the faith to the catechized. Catechists who act as if they are primarily responsible for children's religious formation and can make up for the lack of religious formation in the home are greatly disillusioned.

If a catechist adequately conveys basic Catholic beliefs to the catechized in a prayerful environment, these beliefs are formative in themselves. The degree of formation which occurs, however, often depends upon the support this formation receives in the home.

Catechesis takes place in the midst of a secular world. For this Catholic formation to be effective, parental cooperation is essential. With their cooperation, catechists can touch the minds and hearts of the catechized.

No matter what the circumstances, the Church's basic teachings must be clearly presented by faithful, well-prepared catechists who link their teaching to the whole gamut of Catholic beliefs and practices. Vibrant parishes should support such catechetical efforts as catechists join their efforts with parish service and liturgical ministries.

To conclude our reflections on common sense catechesis, we offer the following suggestions:

- Catechize by making sure that what is taught connects with the lives, secular and religious culture, and the language of the catechized.

- While what is taught remains constant, catechists can be flexible about the approach used. They should always concentrate on basic beliefs and make sure that the catechized learn them.

- Catechetical approaches vary, and there is no one best way to catechize.

- Prayer and Scripture must be integral parts of all catechetical activities.

- When catechizing different ethnic and cultural groups, basic Church teachings remain the same, even though they are presented differently.

- Adult faith formation offers adult learners an opportunity to appreciate and experience ongoing conversion.

- Catechists engage in lifelong learning themselves to facilitate their own continuing conversion.

- Parish catechetical leaders are links between pastors, parents, and other adults, insuring that common sense catechesis happens.

- The *Catechism of the Catholic Church* is a foundation for adult faith formation and catechist certification, and a key resource for common sense catechesis.

- Catechists should use Jesus' story as the foundation on which they balance content and approach in teaching the Good News of God's love, and His special care for the needy and poor.

- Catechists should look to and live out the beatitudes so that their teaching reflects the central message of Jesus.

- Catechists must stress basic Church teachings, making sure that the catechized know them.

- Catechists should use modern technology to catechize, keeping in mind that technology is a tool that must be connected with a living faith community.

Common sense catechesis applies in any situation in which the catechist might be called to teach. This approach takes into account the current culture, presents the basic teachings of the Church, and uses an approach that touches the hearts, souls, and minds of the catechized. In so doing, the catechist teaches the basic beliefs, using language that the catechized understand. At the same time, he or she must remain faithful to the teachings of the *Catechism of the Catholic Church*. The catechist knows that basic teachings are essential aspects of the faith formation of the catechized. With wisdom and prudence, he or she couches the message in age-appropriate language. Each catechetical lesson must fit the intellectual ability, cultural context, family situation, and faith of the catechized.

Finally, the catechist has to remember that the final goal of all catechetical endeavors is to teach the truths of the faith, and to help learners incorporate them into a growing awareness of God's love.

Four words that typify common sense catechesis are "catechist," "culture," "content," and "approach." Keeping them in mind, catechists can mirror the way Jesus catechized when He walked on earth.

CONCLUSION

"The more you unite with Jesus and make him the centre of your life, the more He makes you abandon yourself, decentralize yourself, and open yourself to others."

(Pope Francis, *Address to International Catechetical Congress*, September 27, 2013)

In the twenty-first century, the challenge to effectively catechize invites catechists to examine the meaning of being a Catholic. We should all look at what must be done to teach people the basic truths of the faith in ways that make sense to them. The Church's ability to be true to Jesus' teachings, as she addresses her catechetical challenges, influences her effectiveness in moving people to accept Christ.

In this endeavor, Jesus is the model for all catechetical efforts. He proclaimed the Good News and asked His Church to continue to proclaim it. This ministry demands humility, forgiveness, and patience. Catechists and their directors must recall that no catechetical renewal happens unless the Church centers her ministry on Jesus' message of the kingdom of God. This message touches the spiritual core of every person, where the individual meets God in prayer.

Common sense catechesis begins in our relationship with God. If God did not enter into relationship with us, we could not share Jesus' life and teaching. Our efforts to teach the Good News begin with God's grace. They grow as our life in Christ deepens. They continue through our catechetical preparation and reach fruition in our teachings. The wonderful climax can be seen when the catechized live the message that they learned.

Let the Church's renewal of catechetical ministry focus on prayer, as we remember the words of the *Catechism of the Catholic Church*:

> The drama of prayer is fully revealed to us in the Word who became flesh and dwells among us.... The Son of God who became Son of the Virgin learned to pray according to his human heart. He [learned it from his mother], who kept in her heart ... all the "great things" done by the Almighty. (2598-2599)

We put our catechetical efforts under the guidance of Mary, as Pope John Paul II urged us to do in his apostolic constitution *Fidei Depositum*, which accompanied the release of the *Catechism of the Catholic Church*:

> At the conclusion of this document presenting the *Catechism of the Catholic Church*, I beseech the Blessed Virgin Mary, Mother of the Incarnate Word and Mother of the Church, to support with her powerful intercession the catechetical work of the whole Church on every level, at this time when she is called to a new effort of evangelization." (3)